CW00923034

The Riddle of Nostradamus

PARALLAX RE-VISIONS OF CULTURE AND SOCIETY

Stephen G. Nichols, Gerald Prince, and Wendy Steiner
SERIES EDITORS

The Riddle of Nostradamus

A Critical Dialogue

Georges Dumézil

TRANSLATED BY
Betsy Wing

The Johns Hopkins University Press
Baltimore and London

Originally published as "... *Le moyne noir en gris dedans Varennes,*" © Éditions Gallimard, 1984

 Published 1999
Printed in the United States of America on acid-free paper
9 8 7 6 5 4 3 2 1

The Johns Hopkins University Press
2715 North Charles Street
Baltimore, Maryland 21218-4363

www.press.jhu.edu

Library of Congress Cataloging-in-Publication Data will be found at the end of this book.
A catalog record for this book is available from the British Library.

ISBN 0-8018-6128-4

Contents

Foreword

This book by Georges Dumézil is about Dumézil—about his scholarly methods and even about his life. It is a tour de force application of his methodology. As such, it amounts to a brilliant exercise in comparative method and reconstruction. It is easy to speak here of his methods; to speak of his life will be more difficult.

In this project, Dumézil applies his theoretical models of "exteriorized thinking" (*pensée extériorisée*) to Nostradamus. Why Nostradamus? This obscure sixteenth-century mystic strikes us at first as the most unlikely subject for Dumézil, who spent his academic life developing empirical methods in linguistic approaches to comparative sociology. Dumézil's empiricism involves comparing the institutions of societies linked to one another by way of cognate languages that can be traced back to a prototypical common language, known to linguists as "Indo-European."

The key to this book is the comparative method itself and how this method can reconstruct a frame of mind by externalizing the traditions that formed that frame. If different minds at different times internalize the same given tradition, then a comparatist can find a link between these different minds by examining that tradition in its externalized forms. That is what Dumézil does in linking a tradition he finds reflected in the work of the Roman historian Livy, whose life straddled the first centuries B.C. and A.D., with what went on in the minds of two historical figures who had independently internalized that tradition in the context of their own classical formation. These two figures are Nostradamus, in the sixteenth century A.D., and Louis XVI, in the late eighteenth.

If we look at the tradition as internalized by the minds of Nostradamus and Louis XVI, then it seems as if the opaque verses of Nostradamus, as quoted in the title of Dumézil's book, had prophesied what was actually going on inside the head of Louis XVI at the fatal moments that marked the cataclysmic end of royalty, and of a whole way of life, in revolutionary France. If, however, we look at the tradition as externalized by the comparatist, we can see the opportunities for analogous reactions by two different minds to two analogous historical contingencies—reactions motivated by an analogous mental processing of tradition.

So much for the main thesis of Dumézil's project. But we must address also the medium Dumézil has chosen—that is, a quasi-Platonic narrative, containing dialogues, set in the 1920s. There are historical reasons for Dumézil's choosing this opaque Platonic medium and this equally opaque dramatic setting.

To start with the setting: we cannot easily see through the obscurity of the historical references. Today it would be difficult to find anyone sufficiently knowledgeable to speak with firsthand authority about the relevant history. Further, any effort to discover translucence amid all the opacity could not easily be justified if this book were not what it also is, a brilliant exercise in comparative method and reconstruction.

The little that shows through is this: the book has as one of its subtexts an apologia for Georges Dumézil's rightist past, which is carefully distinguished from the fascist past that came to characterize those of his associates who eventually were involved in Action française. In the end, Dumézil comes across not as a rightist but as a royalist. This self-characterization is relevant to the thoughts purportedly going on inside the head of Louis XVI, the doomed king of a vanishing world, in the forest of Varennes. There are other subtexts as well, involving the demimonde of homosexuality and freemasonry, academic French style, among the elites of the 1920s.

In short, the book has a hidden agenda, much of it expressed in the code of an elitist French upper-class classical education. Even the names are coded. It is as if Dumézil were trying to recover, through encoding, a glimpse of a world that has by now utterly vanished. His stance is not only nostalgic, however: he is clearly striving to highlight those aspects of that world that will allow him to set the record straight, as far as his scholarly and personal reputations are concerned.

The Anglo-American reading public is here faced with a serious intellectual challenge: how to understand the historical context. (And why even bother?) Two most helpful aids are Didier Eribon, *Faut-il brûler Dumézil?* (Flammarion, 1992), and Maurice Olender, *Les langues du paradis: Aryens et Sémites: Un couple providenciel* (Gallimard/Le Seuil, 1989). Both of these works explore the moral as well as the intellectual importance of coming to terms with the problems raised by Dumézil's apologia. They also confront the inherent difficulty of ascertaining the basic facts.

Let us begin with a most striking example, in the person of M. Espopondie, the elderly scholar who emerges as the centerpiece of Dumézil's reminiscences. We find old Espopondie in the act of systematically consigning to the fireplace, piece by piece, evening after evening, a lifetime of accumulated papers. Helping him stoke the fires is the young Dumézil, who portrays himself as the old man's adoring acolyte. With every evening visit, they burn a new stack of papers. Then, one fine evening, they come upon a disquisition Espopondie had once written concerning a set of prophetic verses by Nostradamus, which seem to find their fulfillment in the life of a historical figure from a later era, Louis XVI.

Dumézil is allowed to rescue this disquisition from the fire. He takes it home. He reads and rereads it. From then on, during successive evening visits, the rescued text is discussed and rediscussed, with further elaborations. The evening discussions expand, with other figures joining in. One of the new characters is M. Leslucas.

It so happens that "M. Espopondie," described by Dumézil as a distinguished Orientalist, is a code name for Claude-Eugène Maître, adjunct conservator of the Musée Guimet, who was the first director of the École française d'Extrême-Orient. (This is the man who "discovered" the ruins of Angkor.) Dumézil's book is in turn dedicated to

Henri Sauguet, who was Maître's secretary when the dramatized events took place (Eribon, 171–72). The special relationship Dumézil had with his *maître*, whose real name was Maître, is suggested by the code name he gave to his beloved patron: "Espopondie" plays on the perfect first-person singular of the Latin verb *spondeô, spopondi*, which we may translate as "I solemnly vouch for, having poured a libation" (32).

As for "M. Leslucas," it is a code name for Pierre Gaxotte, to whom Dumézil had dedicated his 1924 book, *Le festin d'immortalité: Étude de mythologie comparée indo-européenne* (Annales du Musée Guimet, vol. 34, Paris); Gaxotte had once been the secretary of Charles Maurras, a key figure in Action française (Eribon, 32).

The Action française of 1924 can hardly be equated with what it later became in the 1930s (33, 83–84), and Dumézil's aloofness from any collaboration with fascist movements has been carefully documented by his defenders (including Eribon [33]). I have no way of knowing for sure, but I trust the judgment of the classicist and historian Pierre Vidal-Naquet, who once told me directly that he thinks Dumézil has been exonerated of all charges and suspicions of collaboration. (Vidal was the scholar who originally recommended to me Eribon's book; Eribon [341] acknowledges Vidal's help.)

The obscurity of a book named after the "black monk in gray" reenacts the obscurity of Dumézil's own hidden life. Amid the grayness, however, are rays of evocation that have shone through to some of his book's most sensitive original readers. In the words of one such reader (Eribon, 172 [my translation]), "It will come as no surprise that Michel Foucault, in a remark reported by Claude Mauriac [*Le temps accompli* (Grasset, 1991), 51], had spontaneously evoked, speaking of Dumézil and of his book on Nostradamus, 'the freemasonic homosexuality of his youth.'" I continue with Eribon's gloss on Foucault's remark (again, my translation): "He [Foucault] means the kind of homosexuality that is a life lived out by belonging to an underground community—a life withdrawn from the gaze of others, in an era that wants that life to be just that way—an era when homosexuals had to advance themselves by wearing masks, simply because homosexuality was forbidden and repressed. It is no doubt in this form of sympathy, founded on a secret kind of complicity [*une complicité secrète*], that one finds the key to many of the stances of Dumézil that would otherwise seem quite incomprehensible."*

The expression "une complicité secrète" has a direct bearing on the even more overtly Platonic appendix to this book, a "divertissement" that seems on the surface an imitation of Plato's *Phaedo*. The main body of the book is opaque enough, but now we confront *obscuriora*. Ironically, however, the more-obscure is more clear, because the model of the ultimate master, Socrates, is overt.

The symbolism of the whole book can now impose itself: Dumézil's memory highlights a few things and shades over many others, just as his master, M. Maître, burns most of his papers and saves only a few choice passages. This book is choice Dumézil.

Gregory Nagy

* "C'est-à-dire l'homosexualité vécue comme l'appartenance souterraine à une communauté, comme une vie dérobée au regard des autres (c'est l'époque qui le veut, une époque où les homosexuels devaient s'avancer masqués, tout simplement parce que l'homosexualité était interdite et réprimée). Il y a sans doute dans cette forme de sympathie fondée sur une complicité secrète la clé de bien des comportements de Dumézil qui pourraient sembler incompréhensibles" (Eribon, *Faut-il brûler Dumézil?* 172).

Preface to the French Edition

to Pierre Nora

Dear Friend,

Because you have kindly induced me to publish these meditations, would you please pass a few bits of useful information on to the reader?

The first part of the book could be called "System of the World, volume 1." But, because neither I nor the generations to come will ever write the volumes that follow, I think a more humble label is better.

It is useless to look for keys. I have constantly mixed memory and fiction. Although my conversation with Gustave Charles Toussaint off Jan Mayen Island is rather meticulously noted, I fear that the characters playing a part in this farce must be somewhat blurred; specifically, the three Perfect Ones must reduce to the only one who is not: after sixty years how could my division of the voices be right? In any case, Espopondie's last winter, as well as our relations, to which he probably owes his name, were indeed as I describe them. Thus the bundle of papers in chapter 2 may be considered authentic. But I must acknowledge that I had not thought of them for a long time—until the end of 1968, when on the third floor of the Princeton Library I took down from the shelves a copy of *Nostradamus* dating from the beginning of the eighteenth century. It was when I reread it, my fingers actually touching the quatrains about "Varennes" and about "Narbon and Saulce," that I thought about the problem again and decided to take it somewhere.

Readers will certainly want to have recourse to the text, and should refer to the two volumes of Le Pelletier's annotated edition, republished in 1976 by Jean de Bonnot, 7, faubourg Saint-Honoré.*

My study would have made little progress if my grandsons and my daughter-in-law had not taken responsibility for a good deal of philological, lexical, statistical, and historical research. The result is that responsibility for the arguments, organization, and conclusions is mine but in large part the worth of the project is due to them.

With sincere thanks,

Georges Dumézil

* This translation makes reference to Charles A. Ward, *The Oracles of Nostradamus* (New York: Charles Scribner and Sons, Modern Library, 1940), as well as to Henry C. Roberts, *The Complete Prophecies of Nostradamus* (New York: Crown, 1994). The translations in general, however, follow Dumézil's interpretation rather than those given by either Ward (closer to Le Pelletier's) or Roberts. [Trans.]

". . . the Black Monk in Gray within Varennes"

A Nostradamian Farce

For Henri Sauguet,
in memory of Roger Désormière
and Claude-Eugène Maître

1

About sixty years ago, between 1922 and 1925, I had the good fortune to become close friends with M. Espopondie, one of the men who has influenced me most deeply and, I believe, most productively. I was enjoying being twenty-five and he was nearing fifty. The battles of 1918 had somewhat shaped and humanized me, pulling me from the microcosm of *khâgnes* and books—indeed exciting, but unreal—to plunge me abruptly into the mixture of hell and paradise that the episodes of everyday life in an army campaign were for a young second lieutenant in the artillery. The words on the pall of Captain Cartesius, "I reflected little; I lived," did not apply. On the contrary, the principal lines of my thought and my behavior were permanently delineated during the years I knew Espopondie, especially the last year.

An itinerant scholar and administrator, like many of our great Orientalists at the beginning of this century, he had long haunted the most distant parts of Asia. This was the opening that brought me—just beginning my studies—into contact with him. My Orient was not the same as his, but we held part of India in condominium. At that time I was also beginning to sketch out my first ideas, with all their illusions, concerning the Indo-Europeans and comparative mythology, and that interested him. Very soon, however, this no longer formed the center of our relationship. He was equally fond of poetry, music, and the plastic arts, and he had read prodigiously and lived intensely. His education as a philosopher gave him a kindly mastery of this great quantity of knowledge and experience. I went to avant-garde concerts and wrestling matches with him, and we visited Belgian museums. Every time something that I had not yet imagined would become clear.

But it was especially after the autumn of 1924 and during the final winter of his life that I truly came to know him. I was aware that, since his return to France just before the war, his health had not been good. I then learned that he suffered from two ailments, and the differing treatments for the two could not be reconciled. One of these affected his heart. In October the attacks came one after the other, and sometimes Espopondie remained indoors for weeks. Soon he became certain that his end was near, and he wished to make his departure wisely. He found he had reached a point at which he could look back on his life with neither smugness nor regret. He had had the "weakness," as he called it, feigning humility, to save packets of letters, some of them extremely intimate (he had passed through a number of stormy periods), as well as bundles of notes, notebooks, and books begun and then abandoned (he had published very little). He wanted, before destroying them, to take one last trip among these ultimate expressions—whether ridiculous or remarkable—of his thoughts, his research, and, if not his passions, at least some sincere attachments and many mirages of sentiment. He had, no doubt, put me to the test and decided that I inspired confidence. Also I probably provided some slight compensation for the grief he felt, and had once confessed to me, that he would die without leaving a son. In any case, he suggested that I join him on this pilgrimage and in this holocaust.

Around six o'clock almost every evening, when his secretary left, I would go to his place. We chatted while his servant provided us with a light supper; then we would move over to the fire that he always kept burning in his little study. He sat down in his armchair, sometimes slightly out of breath (occasionally I would be worried), but often very comfortably. I would then go into one of the three rooms where, next to the books, there lay several large envelopes still containing the ghosts of his life. He would read the letters or have me read them. Sometimes a photograph would emerge and he would look at it for a few seconds, and then give it back to me. All of this went into the fire, and it never occurred to me to hold any back. He was so detached as he glanced through whole folders of reading notes, reflections, or projects and consigned them to the void. Only rarely would he ask me to read them to him. He would see how this or that page of writing related to some preoccupation, later forgotten, and tell me simply, "Keep going."

One evening, however, when Espopondie seemed less tired than usual, I pulled fifteen or so pages out of a long envelope. They were collected in a notebook with a title that intrigued me: "Prolegomena to Some Possible Secondary Physics."

"I'm glad to have found this old commentary," Espopondie said, smiling. "It must go back to the first years of this century, when I was your age. Put it aside and go on."

The rest of the envelope was tossed with the usual simplicity; then Espopondie motioned to me to pick up the notebook again.

I knew where Espopondie stood on the subject of metaphysics. He was fascinated by research on the atom, then just in its infancy, and he seemed to foresee its rapid development. "They were a little hasty when they called the atom 'the atom'—that is, the indivisible," he remarked. "You'll see, they'll break it in pieces, and then every piece into pieces. Infinitely, maybe. The Eleatics will get hold of it." And what did he expect from philosophy? Some days a lot, perhaps. Sometimes little or nothing. Was he a materialist? He avoided any such big words or partisan positions. In any case, he stuck to experience, refusing to separate what is habitually called *spirit* from what is called *matter*. He often told me that he had never felt anything resembling the famous religious anxiety. Born into a family of disbelievers who were, I think, anticlerical, he had not been baptized and had not had to break away from the faith of his childhood. Rather, during his youth, and especially when he was a student on the rue d'Ulm, it had required all of his intelligence and intense love for freedom not to let himself be swept away in the floods of antireligious fervor incited by Émile Combes. Moreover, he admired and loved theologies as he did all of humanity's creations, but he saw the artifice in all of them. He would willingly have come to the defense of established religions as long as they served as the refuge of the weak and desperate, but, rightly or wrongly, he thought he more frequently saw in them intolerance and abdication.

Would I say he was agnostic? He was convinced that the advances of physics, whose rhythms he marked, and the advances of critical history, to which he had contributed, would put an end to many empty formulas. At the same time, however, he foresaw that, as with the atom, in replacing the illusions of the past this work would give rise to other views that would waste no time in proving to be equally illusory or insufficient. A rationalist? Yes, certainly. He was even quite prepared to deify reason. But there were two attitudes, or rather two varieties of the same attitude, that struck him as blasphemy against this goddess. Under the pretext of shying away from the irrational, he said, some people refuse to record any observation that the state of our knowledge does not allow us to interpret, and others fail to understand the mystery of the evolution relentlessly transforming apparently the most stable organic equilibriums into other forms of equilibrium that are no less temporary. To the first he recalled the objection raised, despite the evidence of the sea's horizon, against those who said the earth is round: how could men in the antipodes walk upside down? He advised the second group to ponder the evolution that began first on some spot on the skin that was sensitive to light and went on to produce the structure of the mammalian eye, which then, over a period of several centuries, with the collaboration of the entire human brain, now extends into opticians' and photographers' equipment, itself in a process of ceaseless transformation.

All this, of course, can be—or will be able to be—put into equations and justified by natural selection, but how can one not *also* suspect that from the beginning, and for each one of the billions of attendant and convergent changes that took place, there was the equivalent of a project? In short, his rationalism did not lock him into the present for either the means or the matter of his study. He entrusted the future with the progressive explanation of the unexplained, without imagining that this should ever be completed. Many stubborn errors of assertion and denial, he went on, are the result of some good minds in each generation having claimed to do the work of twenty or a hundred and claiming, at the same time, that they have put their finger on the "heart of the matter."

This portrait of him would be incomplete if I did not mention that he had no fear of and no curiosity about death, the most comprehensible of phenomena. He did not think that anything of him would survive the decomposition of his brain. His fondness for beautiful things made him hope that his death would come peacefully and neatly, but he knew that the two illnesses fighting it out in his thorax made this unlikely.

I have made this necessary detour to explain the interest that this pragmatic mind in its youth had in a few lines of the *Oracles* of Michel de Nostradamus. He made the interest, apparently revived this evening, clear to me in a few words.

"All the experiences we call psychic, all the notable cases of thought transmission and premonition, especially when there is communication with the beyond or with supernatural beings, run up against the same obstacle: no matter how honest the observer, no matter how strict the controls, there always remains the suspicion that this is autosuggestion—collective delusion, and usually trickery. Prediction of the future, whether near or distant, uttered by a 'seer' seems to avoid this fate, at least when it has been written down at a known date in a *ne varietur* form and consequently been shielded from the favors of oral transmission. One can suppose that history, whether in the short or the long run, will either verify or refute it—with, however, the following qualifications: that there is no limit to history and that, unless the predicted event is dated, there is always the chance that each generation will consider the event to be reserved for the future. But there are not many such records, and those that exist do not lend themselves, or lend themselves too well, to this a posteriori test: whether too general, or incoherent, or ambiguous, or all three at once, they bring to mind several, even numerous events over the centuries, each of which can be adjusted to their formulation if one gives it a good try.

"Nostradamus's *Centuries* is not exempt from this condition. All one has to do is skim through the commentaries written on it for more than three hundred years. Actually, all one has to do is read it to throw in the towel—with the exception of a very few quatrains in which enigma plays a limited role and precise details about people or places are given; by this I mean the rare proper names, improbable in the mathematical sense, that have afterward emerged only once in history as actors or settings. The most famous case is the twentieth quatrain of century 9, where not only all the exegetes but even the most skeptical of readers cannot help experiencing the astonishing feeling that Nostradamus has outlined the dramatic events of Varennes with their tragic consequences—the ill-considered trip that, almost two and a half centuries later, was to lead the last divine-right king and his family down the blind alley of a small town in the Argonne. Look at the beginning of my paper; I must have cited the quatrain."

He had indeed transcribed it in the very first lines. I read:

De nuict viendra par la forest de Reines,
Deux pars vaultorte Herne la pierre blanche.
Le moyne noir en gris dedans Varennes,
Esleu cap cause tempeste, feu sang tranche.

(By night shall come through the forest of Reines
Two parts, face about, the queen a white stone,
The black monk in gray within Varennes.
Chosen cap causes tempest, fire, blood, slice.)

I knew the quatrain. More than once I had been intrigued by Nostradamus, but I had always ended up putting down the book.

"It is getting a bit late for us to read the paper tonight," Espopondie said. "Take it with you."

I had qualms about reading alone these pages that clearly meant so much to him. I made excuses and said I would rather give it some thought first. Espopondie then offered to lend me the annotated edition provided by Anatole Le Pelletier in 1867. But this was unnecessary. I had it at home, inherited from my grandfather, and it was the only one in which I had read Nostradamus. Following the composite copy in the Bibliothèque nationale, it carefully reproduces Pierre Rigaud's first edition (*Centuries* 1–7, Lyon, 1558?; 8–10, 1566), and in the notes it gives the variant versions from the second edition, by Benoist Rigaud (whose kinship to Pierre is unknown) (Lyon, 1568). Le Pelletier also provides an intelligible paraphrase for a great many of the quatrains, as well as notes in which he confidently and naively makes use of the commentary of his numerous predecessors, but especially of his own erudition and his own flashes of inspiration.

"Good. Isn't it tomorrow that our friends are coming?"

After having much savored the world, Espopondie had of necessity withdrawn from it, but he made a few exceptions to his solitude. Ever since he had become more gravely ill, twice a week he received—together we received—two young men, both very intelligent but entirely different, whom I had quickly taken to. Espopondie said that these evening gatherings made him think of the *Phaedo*.

"So together you can decipher my paper. You will read it to them. Knowing them, I am sure they will have something useful to say. Afterward, we'll decide on the fate of these pages. They will go into the fire, or if one of you finds them interesting, he will take them."

It was nearly midnight when I left Espopondie. He was peaceful and relieved, I thought, the way a king would be the evening of his abdication. I myself slept extremely well, and the next morning I found my Le Pelletier—not without difficulty, for it was not conspicuous. Reading through his commentary and notes, I wondered what our friend had been able to get from such a text. Yes, it did concern a character, apparently important, who "shall come at night within

Varennes." And yes, the final line predicts that because of a "chosen cap" (*cap* is not followed by a period in 1566, but it is in 1568), there will be instances of great violence, and even at the end a "slice," a blade that—after the fire and blood—makes one think of the wise Guillotin's humanitarian invention. But what relationship did all the rest have to the dramatic events of Varennes? As for Le Pelletier's glosses, although one translated the word *slice* well and another opportunely recalled that the king, for his clandestine journey, had put on a gray habit like the character in the quatrain, on the whole his comments were astounding, and his use of Greek and Latin made things worse, not better. This is what I copied:

(line a) at "forest de Reines": Latin *fores* 'door' (it is a question, therefore, of a concealed door in the queen's apartments through which the royal couple secretly left the Tuileries).

(line b) at "deux pars": *part,* an old word for "spouse, husband or wife."

(line b) at "vaultorte": Romance; composite word from *vaulx* 'valley' and *torte* 'tortuous,' that is, a crooked road or indirect path (it is a question of the change of direction decided upon by the king as he left Sainte-Menehould: toward Varennes rather than, as originally planned, toward Verdun).

(line b) at "Herne": first, Greek *ernos* 'stem, offshoot'; Herne, anagram for *reine* [queen], by metaplasm changing the *h* into *i*.

(line b) at "pierre blanche": the queen, a precious stone [*pierre*] dressed in white [*blanche*].

(line c) at "moyne": Greek *monos* 'alone, abandoned.'

(line c) at "noir": anagram for *roi* [king], by apheresis, by cutting the *n*.

(line d) at "esleu": Romance *élu* [chosen].

(line d) at "cap": by apocope *Cap.* for *Capet.* Benoist Rigaud puts a period, marking an abbreviation, after Cap, which is not there in Pierre Rigaud's version.

(line d) at "esleu cap": *Capet élu,* that is, the transformation of the ancient absolute royalty of the Capetians into an elective or constitutional monarchy.

Once again I felt the impatience that an earlier reading, a number of years before, had caused in me when I met up with this ill-advised

Greek and Latin, this pretentious paraphernalia of metaplasm, apheresis, apocope, this refusal to accept the clearest words, *forest*, *monk*, *black*, in their ordinary sense. And the geography! The history! The road from Sainte-Menehould to Varennes is neither tortuous nor crooked nor indirect. Constitutional monarchy is not elective; never, not in 1791 nor at the moment of flight nor later, would there ever be any question of "electing" a king as was done in Poland or in the Holy Roman Empire at the death of a pope. The king, who had become suspect, restored to power without election, was simply requested as the dynasty's representative to commit himself to respect the constitution. And that "Capet" reduced to "cap," with or without a period! It did not take me long, leafing through the *Centuries*, to come up with a "Cap de Byzance," which could hardly be a Capetian.

So I was curious to see how Espopondie had treated these four lines when I returned late in the afternoon to his place.

I shall not go on at length now about the interlocutors I met with every week. It suffices to say that M. de Momordy was a brilliant young diplomat freshly graduated from the Grand Concours, who now awaited a post in the Near East, and that Charles Leslucas, at twenty-two only slightly younger than he, had been my classmate at the École Normale Supérieure and that he was beginning a career in archaeology. He too was interested in the Eastern Mediterranean, but in its past.

As soon as we were all together, Espopondie filled the others in about our discovery; then I began to read the paper he had written in 1902. It was easy: our friend had always had the clear and elegant handwriting with which we were familiar. Here is what we heard.

2

Above all, at the risk of seeming to force a first and wide-open door, I must analyze the feeling that I myself, like many previous readers, have that there is a connection—I purposely use the vaguest word—between what is said in the quatrain and what is commonly referred to as "the drama of Varennes."

First point: no city, no village in France named Varennes has ever played a role in our history except, during a single night in 1791, the small town of Varennes-en-Argonne. Up to that moment it had been so obscure that, when news of the king's arrest reached the Assembly, most of the deputies had never heard of the name.

Second point: the action described in the first three lines of the quatrain is insignificant in itself, but in this very insignificance it is precise. Both its content and its limits tally with the brief event of 1791. What then is this action?

Grammatically, despite punctuation that is simultaneously arbitrary and mechanical, as it frequently is in the Centuries, *the second line forms a parenthesis set like a foreign body within the main sentence constituted by line 1, which contains a subjectless verb, and line 3, which contains a verbless subject. Laid end to end, these two segments give the following: "A certain individual—designated by the puzzling periphrasis 'the black monk'—dressed in gray will come at night into Varennes, after having passed through a certain forest—enigmatically called 'the forest of Reines' [the forest of queens]." The action therefore amounts to nothing more than "coming within Varennes" at the end of a journey. This, in fact, is the only action of the king, his sole connection with Varennes during this night that will seal his doom. He does not make his "entrance" into the town either as a sovereign or as a conqueror, as, in fact, other characters do whom the quatrains describe as "entering." He simply "comes" because Varennes is a relay post on his rashly modified itinerary, a stop he counts on going beyond without mishap just as he has done with all the others. But Varennes, in a state of alert, is a blind alley. The king can "come within," but only like game entering a trap. He "comes within," but his only alternative for "leaving" is to be forcibly returned to where he started.*

Two further details emphasize this impression of similarity: the action takes place "by night" and the character is "in gray." Now the royal family, having left Paris during the night of June 20–21, did indeed arrive at the relay post of Varennes the following night, precisely at 10:45, and witnesses are in agreement that the king's disguise, indeed, consisted of a gray habit and an ordinary wig; likewise the queen was wearing a dress of gray silk and a gray hat. These two similarities, however, do not carry the same weight. In the Centuries *there are at least twenty events that take place "by night," which is natural because the nighttime suits the violent acts that fill its pages; moreover, the phrase "by night" is placed, as it is here, at the beginning of a line about ten times and in four instances at the beginning of a quatrain. If, therefore, Nostradamus made up the event, these words that were familiar to his pen could easily come to mind and could only have pleased him, because they situate the scene in a more fantastic, not to say romantic, setting. The result is that this correspondence has only a negative value, in the sense that disagreement on this point would have spared one from continuing the inquiry. The gray habit, on the other hand, like the "black monk," is even more interesting, if I may say so, because the "gray" note, close as it is to "black" yet somewhat belying it, certainly is supposed to be meaningful.*

Third and most important point: the relationship of the fourth line to the three preceding ones. This "coming within Varennes" is apparently harmless, just as Louis XVI, at least in the first few moments, could have believed that the arrival of his carriage in this place presented no danger. But, like the arrival of Louis XVI, the black monk's "coming" is followed by horrifying events immediately enumerated in the line that follows, as if to suggest that they are its consequence. This line, grammatically correct, is instantly clear to a reader in our century, except its first two words: a certain agent called "élu cap[.]" provokes a tempest—obviously political rather than meteorological, to judge by what follows—with fires, spilled blood, and, when we come to the final syllable of the line, the blade, because "le tranche" is specifically a chisel of tempered steel used to strike and cut either heated or cold iron. These four words (tempest, fire, blood, blade) *provide a good, pithy summary of what will take place in the nineteen months that follow the few hours of trouble at Varennes. They are, moreover, in conformity with a type of enumeration frequently found in the* Centuries, *particularly when the author wants to lay out different aspects or moments of a public calamity, and* fire *and* blood *appear together several times. But it is here alone that the most original word,* blade, *appears.*

What, then, is this "esleu cap[.]" that will be the cause of these violent events? An examination of the vocabulary used by Nostradamus, which is strange sometimes but constant in its choices, permits a response.

In the Centuries, esleu *(and the same is true of* élection *and* électeur*) conforms to our technical and political understanding of this word and means only one thing: "chosen from among candidates by electors as lay or religious head." There are at least twenty examples, such as:*

> *3.41a: Bossu sera esleu par le conseil.*
> (Crookback shall be elected by the council.)
> *3.55b: Le jour après sera esleu Pontife.*
> (The day after shall be elected Pontiff.)
> *4.47c: esleu du peuple*
> (elected by the people)
> *5.56a–b: Par le trespas du très-vieillard Pontife*
> *Sera esleu Romain de bon aage.*
> (Through the death of the very-old-man Pontiff
> A Roman of good age shall be elected.)

As for the substantive cap[.], *if I have counted correctly, in the entire text of the* Centuries, *only three other examples of this exist, two of which, like this, are in the ninth. In all three instances the meaning is certain: head.*

In 9.30c, a certain "cap de Bisance" [head of Bisance] cries out "alas" in the streets, then seems to receive "aid from Gaddes"—an important person, needless to say, and no doubt the Ottoman sultan, the same character designated in 4.38b as "Byzantine head [chef] *captive in Samothrace" and described in 10.62c–d: "Byzantine head* [chef] *Sallon de Sclavonia, / Shall come convert them to the law of the Arabs." This title is reminiscent of 8.39a–c, where the three verses concern a "Byzantine prince, prince of Tholouses, head* [chef] *Tholentin."*

According to 9.64d, an invader will cross the Pyrenees and will occupy Narbonne without meeting resistance; "By sea and land are greatest efforts made / Cap. having no secure land to stay in." This unfortunate "cap." has less luck than the "head" [chef] *described in 1.98d as "The fleeing head saved in a sea barn."*

Quatrain 7.37 is an inextricable tangle concerning a naval event. It contains the word chef *twice (a and c) and the word* cap. *once (d). It is more than likely that the threatened "head"* [chef] *of the boat (a) is the same as the "cap" that comes after the word* boats *(d) and who seems to be swallowed up by the sea.*

The word chef, *very frequently used in the* Centuries, *most often is the equivalent of "political or military head." It is only very rarely to be taken in the physical sense of "head" (as in 6.92d). But politically it can be the abstract designation of the highest position in a political body, the supreme power. Thus:*

> *6.70a: Au chef du monde le grand Chyren sera.*
> (The great Chyren will belong to the world power.)
> *8.65d: Il parviendra au chef de son empire*
> *Vingt mois tiendra le règne à grand pouvoir.*
> (He will attain the leadership of his empire
> For twenty months will rule with great power.)

Considering how ignorant we are of the methods of composition of the Centuries, *it would be foolish to pretend we could discover why, in a few lines,* cap *was preferable to* chef. *There is another distinctive feature, on the other hand, that is more comprehensible. In 9.20d (that is, in our stanza), and in 9.30c (with a capital C because it is at the beginning of the line), the 1566 edition, by Pierre Rigaud, writes* cap *with no period and the 1568 edition, by Benoist Rigaud, adds the period, indicating an abbreviation:* cap. *In 9.64d (with a capital C at the beginning of the line), both editions write* cap., *whereas in 7.37d neither one has a period. No doubt the author, or editor, or someone revising the text, without making reference to etymology, without thinking, for example, of "cap d'escouade" [squad captain]—the equivalent of "caporel" [lance corporal] during the reign of François I—considered* cap *to be the abbreviation for* capitaine *[captain], a word Nostradamus also used occasionally in the general sense of "head." He did so once, in particular, in the same century, 9.90a: "Un capitaine de la Grand Germanie" [A leader of Great Germany], and twice in 7 (9a, 28d).*

Conclusion: the "esleu cap" in 9.20d is either the individual "head" or the superior organ, "power," created by election. The invasive legislature, the sovereign Convention, or one of its members (Robespierre would then be the best candidate) corresponds to this definition. The "coming within Varennes" of the "black monk" necessitates that the author of the quatrain will not only conjure up a bloody revolution but assert that this revolution was caused by a power resulting from elections. We are consequently, and with new information, sent back to the events that filled the final months of the life of Louis XVI. It is improbable that some other coming of some other man in gray within some other Varennes has ever conformed to the structure of this evocation.

These conformities, immediately perceptible, make it impossible for us to leave the groups of words that create an enigma in the first three lines to their mystery. We must look to see if the circumstances of the events of 1791 do not uncover the meaning that the words themselves do not provide at first glance. Why is the principal character disguised beneath the periphrasis "the black monk"? What is this "forest of Reines" through which he comes into Varennes, and which is a sufficiently important point in his itinerary that it is the only one mentioned? Finally, what is the meaning of the dense information, with no apparent syntax, provided by the second line?

Espopondie interrupted me. "Perhaps there is not enough emphasis in my paper on the difference between how the first part, which you have just read, is argued and what is to follow. Up to now we have only considered the parts written not only in ordinary French, but clearly, without mystery or metaphor, and therefore not requiring reflection; to understand, it is enough to accept the words in their ordinary sense. From now on we shall be dealing with the two elements of the long sentence composed of lines a and c—the forest of Reines and the black monk—which, although they, too, are written in the most ordinary French, although they each have a certain and simple function in the grammar of the sentence, are willfully enigmatic. They do not state; rather, they suggest what they have to say, and they require a key. Now this key, if we assume that the whole is coherent, can only be in what we have already obtained: the 'similarity' we have just defined and analyzed between the elements that are clear in the same lines and the occurrence of June 1791. Moreover, right at the point where I interrupted your reading, there is a third question, which my paper seems to link to the examination of the first two as if it were of the same nature, but it is, in reality, heterogeneous. Not only is the parenthesis constituting the second line not clear either in its elements or in how they fit, but it is not even written in ordinary language—in a French that can be construed. I shall get back to this when we come to this third question, in the second line. But let us be clear that first we must finish elucidating what seems to be a unified sentence in which the second line is only a parasitic guest. Will you go on?"

I started to read again:

A few reflections on what happened between Paris and Varennes, between dawn on June 21, 1791, and the night of June 21–22, make it all comprehensible.

The royal family, which had left the Tuileries in small groups during the first part of the night of June 20–21, reassembled outside the Saint-Martin gate in a berline, the carriage that was to take the group to Lorraine. The Swedish count, Axel de Fersen, who had vowed his chivalrous devotion to the queen, organized it all and occupied the coachman's seat as far as the relay post at Bondy, on the edge of the famous "forest."

At Bondy, around three in the morning, according to plan—and after the delicate part of it, fortunately, seemed to have been successfully completed—the occupants of the berline separated into two groups. *On the one hand, Fersen, on horseback, followed at a distance by his valet,* turned tail *toward the northwest, then diagonally toward the northeast, and thus,* cutting all the valleys, *reached Mons, in Belgium, where he expected to meet his protégés again very shortly. The royal family, on the other hand, continued its journey directly to the east. The berline, driven from that point on by a French gentleman preceded and flanked by postilions, reached, without incident, and crossed between midday and the evening, the interminable,* whitish landscape of chalky Champagne. *Therefore, given the history, Bondy, rather than the first relay post, is the real point of departure for the adventure.*

Although we must not reconstitute from ifs and conditionals a history that did not take place, it is possible to conjecture that this separation at Bondy, over and above the grief it was bound to have caused the queen, contributed also to the failure of the enterprise. The dangers they believed they had left behind in getting out of Paris awaited the berline at Sainte-Menehould, in the person of young Drouet, the son of the man in charge of the relay post. And if the Swede had held the reins to the end of the journey, he would not easily have agreed to the bad maneuver the king forced his replacement to make. Certainly, he would not have changed the itinerary and would not have driven the berline into the blind alley of Varennes instead of going on to reach Verdun.

The curtain calls of history can be strange. In this same area, more than a thousand years earlier, during a hunting party through the same forested plateau, even perhaps in the spot called "forêt de Bondy," one of the last Merovingians, Childéric II, was assassinated by conspiring vassals who also killed his wife, the queen, Blitilde (or Bilichilde). His crime was attempting to take back the power usurped by the mayors of the palace. A final and futile effort: following this double murder, it did not take the first race long to vanish in the shadow of the second, the Carolingians. That night in 1791 the Capetian queen, the soul of royal and royalist resistance, had no time to think about the fate of Blitilde and the Merovingians. Nor, when they stopped at Bondy, could she foresee that a few months later it would be by the blade that she and the king would end the adventure in which her friend Fersen had enlisted her and her family, in the hope of rebuilding a royal power more and more diminished by assemblies and factions. But such was history.

The next night the journey was cut short. An hour before midnight, the berline entered Varennes. *The king, announced by Drouet, was quickly identified, taken into custody, and forced to return. The following year the Convention—the first assembly* elected *by the people, now sovereign as a result of the new constitution—would abolish the royalty, and first tolerate and then organize violence:* cannons *in the courtyard of the Louvre, the* massacre *of the Swiss Guards, then every degree of the* terror. *The royal family would await its fate at the Temple, in the convent-fortress that first had sheltered the soldier monks wearing the white robes with red crosses, and that Philip the Fair (after trying and burning the Knights Templar at the stake) turned over to a related order, the Hospitalers of Saint Jean of Jerusalem, the* soldier-monks wearing the black robe *with a white cross. On January 21, 1793, as the finishing touch, the* blade *would fall on the Temple's inmate. The queen would still have nine months to live.*

The words and groups of words I have emphasized in the text provide the answer to the unresolved questions.

1. By designating the fugitive with the periphrasis "the black monk," the quatrain announces and anticipates the end of the adventure in progress; it projects the consequence into the cause, the captivity in the Temple into the defeat at Varennes: Louis XVI, demeaned, the pathetic heir of the black-robed soldier-monks, will soon—and until his sentencing—inhabit the Temple.

The juxtaposition of black *and* gray *in the third line is obviously intentional. The costume chosen by the king for his flight was gray, but by evoking, beyond this, his coming imprisonment by the color of the robes of the usual occupants of the Temple, by thus flinging onto the shoulders of the king a second cloak, one no less foreign to his function, the quatrain forces upon us, in almost plain language, the image, the very idea, of* disguise, *and gives a tragic turn to the futile masquerade of 1791. Louis XVI is no longer a poor man in the Tuileries; he is already the martyr disguised in the gray costume worn in the berline.*

2. Although it is the approaching future that justifies that the king be, if one may say so, onomastically disguised as a "black monk," it is the past, a recollection more than a thousand years old, connected to the event in progress, that makes the forest of Bondy deserve to be called "la forêt de Reines"—the forest of queens. The fate of the Merovingian queen killed there prefigured the fate awaiting, with a few more formalities, the Capetian queen. "Queens" . . . a plural fraught with history's harmonies. Framed thus by these two allusions to the symmetrical fates of two dynasties—Bondy, the Temple—"coming within Varennes" takes on a sense of heavy doom that saves it from mediocrity and makes it worthy of Aeschylus or Shakespeare.

Furthermore, although it is indeed the king first and foremost, the royal power, who is in question here, and consequently it is definitely the king who, with his family subsumed somehow beneath his primacy, "will come within Varennes," nonetheless, from the first line, the allusion to "the forest of queens" places Marie-Antoinette in her real role again. More energetic and intelligent than her husband, supported by the personal devotion she inspired in Fersen, although the quatrain does not even name her, she was the inspiration for this final effort to restore royal power. The conjuring up of the first "queen of Bondy" just when she herself is going to join her ghost, in short, plays the same role in the quatrain as the astonishing feminine element floating, with no grammatical authorization, at the end of the "Cantique de saint Jean." Mallarmé has the headless prophet say:

Illuminée au même
Principe qui m'élut,
Penche un salut.

(Illuminated by the same
Principle that chose me,
She/It nods in greeting.)*

Mallarmé thereby makes it understood that the main character in his tragedy is not John the Baptist, but she whom he does not even name, Herodias, the murderess who is not satisfied in her cruelty and who is vulnerable to grace. This all takes place as if both poets, differently but equally affected by preciosity, used an apparently pointless detail to insinuate the essential element that they could not or would not make manifest.

Espopondie signaled me to stop reading. "Excuse me for interrupting you, but I want to repeat and emphasize, more than this old paper of mine does, that what still remains before us, the exegesis of the last obscure bit of the quatrain, the second line, will be undertaken under new conditions. After having analyzed elements with correct syntax and clear meaning, and others whose syntax is also correct but which are written in the form of enigmas, we are now going to find ourselves confronted by a series of elements, none of which except one seems enigmatic. Each one of them seems to mean something straightforward in the ordinary French of the period, but they elude any grammatical construction, thus increasing the complexity of the lock on this last cubbyhole. But our dowry of keys is also richer. Will you continue?"

I started to read again.

3. These remarks justify the importance given by the quatrain to the "forest of queens" and consequently to what happened that day at Bondy: the separation of Fersen and the royal family. At the same time that this deprived the travelers of their best—their only—adviser, it must have

* A curious note of interpretation—particularly because Dumézil's subject is interpretation: the feminine element "illuminated" here is usually construed as the head [*la tête*] of John the Baptist, although perhaps, under such dire circumstances, for the "headless prophet" any feminine element must first be Herodias. [Trans.]

deeply upset the queen. Now there has to be something in the quatrain that registers, that indicates, Bondy's importance in this manner, something not merely geographical and historical in nature, but sentimental and dramatic. What can this "something" be if not the parenthesis, the second line that, like parentheses in general, can only be called for—as a sort of gloss—by the words immediately preceding it: "through the forest of queens, hints the author, and this is why I am recalling this one alone of all the relay posts on the journey"?

The line is written in the extremely elliptical language, with no syntax and no liaisons, that is frequently employed in the Centuries. *It is made up of four notations, four phrases that stand alone, each of which may be the equivalent of a sentence, dropped onto the paper: (a) "deux parts," (b) "vaultorte," (c) "Herne," (d) "la pierre blanche." We are not without resources to deal with the first and the last.*

(a) What took place in the "forest of queens," the "bipartition" of the formerly unified group of travelers, had precisely this result: it replaced the single group with two later groups, "deux parts"—two parts. The turn of phrase fits because the language of Nostradamus never uses partie, *or* parti, *but frequently designates humans in groups that result from a broken unit by the simple word* part.

(d) "La pierre blanche" could be a place; it is not. But we know the itinerary followed by the berline after *the "bipartition" of its occupants. Soon, and for hours on end, practically until they arrived at Argonne, the royal family—amputated, if we may call it that, following Fersen's removal—would have nothing to contemplate to the right or to the left except the whiteness of the ground, the chalky monotony of Champagne.*

Lacking the grammatical articulation denied us, when we compare these two findings a logical linkage is suggested for the entire line, with the exception of "Herne": (a) "two parts" (are created), (b) (one part defined as) "vaultorte," (d) (the other characterized or symbolized by the dominant landscape of its journey), "the white rock." And this symmetrical structure in turn suggests that the adjective (or participle) vaultorte, *balancing "the white rock," provides information of the same sort; that is, it is an indication of the itinerary that the "first part," Fersen himself, the part that separated from the royal family at Bondy, will follow. And in fact, this composite is of a known sort; it is suited to fulfilling this function and it seems incapable of fulfilling any other.*

Vaultorte *is in the feminine singular. It is thus directly attached to the first "part"* [la part]. *This is the only part still available, the part deduced from the preceding plural—or rather, dual (unless it directly attaches to the road* [la route] *that this "part" will follow), because the very existence of the two "parts" only makes sense in view of the divergent directions they will take.*

The word is composed of vaul[x] *and the feminine* torte, *well attested in Old French along with* torse. *This participle most frequently refers to spiral torsion and, therefore, to three-dimensional space (*fil tors *[twisted thread];* Colonne torse *[wreathed column];* Alain Barbe-Torte *[Alain Twisted-Beard]). Here it is only playing on the two dimensions of the earth's surface or of a road map and, because it concerns an itinerary, it must be slanted more toward "turning" than toward "torsion."* Tort[e] *must be the equivalent of its barbaric doublet, one of those hideous Low Latin participles ending in* utus, tortu[e], *defined in the old Larousse as "partially deviating from a straight direction or its natural direction." Nostradamus himself uses it in this sense (5.75d), giving the name "baston tortu" to a twisted stick that is either the bishop's crosier or, rather, I believe, the curved lituus of Roman augurs.*

Let us go back to the bipartition at Bondy at dawn on June 21. While the royal family kept traveling more or less in a straight line toward the east, continuing the route already traversed from Paris, Fersen began to wind along the great turns that would take him to Mons. These were more than just bends—the first stage led him back a full quarter-turn—but because he did not want to be seen in Paris, the rider went around the city and galloped toward the northwest as far as Le Bourget, where he rejoined the Valenciennes road, changing his course once again toward the northeast.

As for vaul[x], *there is no reason to deprive it of its most specific sense —valley(s). When the royal family left Bondy it went up the Marne Valley, but his "winding" took Fersen from valley to valley on his way to Belgium. He crossed the successive basins of the Rivers Oise, Somme, and Sambre to reach Senlis at eight o'clock, Compiègne at noon, Noyon at two o'clock, Ham at four, and Saint-Quentin before six. From there he took a shortcut to reach Le Cateau, went through Landrecies at night, stopped over at Quesnoy, avoided Valenciennes, a garrison where he might have been recognized, and left France at Bavay, not far from Mons.*

Finally, the linking of the two words in vaul[x]-torte *belongs to a type of free construction that Nostradamus liked to use, usually doing so, moreover, with two words: an appointed substantive provides information about the circumstances (time, place, manner . . .) concerning a participle and sometimes an infinitive. Thus, compared with the analytic, explicit construction that we have, for example, in*

> *4.9b: sera blessé* aux *cuisses*
> (will be wounded *in* the thighs)
> *7.20c:* de *sang chappelle teincte*
> (*with* blood chapel stained)
> *8.59d:* par *mer chassé, etc.*
> (pursued *by* sea, etc.)

we read:

> *6.36d: Roy nuict blessé*
> (King wounded *during* the night)
> *10.30c: Cap de Bisance rues crier helas*
> (Head of Bisance to cry alas *through* the streets)
> *9.100a: Navalle pugne nuit sera supérée*
> (Naval battle shall be won *at* night)
> *10.49d: Beuvant par force eaux souphre envenimées*
> (Forcibly drinking waters poisoned *with* sulphur)

The same construction can be found with a word inserted:

> *3.29b: terre peres tombez*
> (their fathers fallen *to* the ground)

Or even reversed:

> *3.10d: Le grand, mené croc en ferree cage*
> (The great man, led *by* hook into an iron cage)

Likewise, vaultorte, *which could equally well be written* vaulx torte, *means "curved* through *the valleys." This sort of compound word was much in use during the last years of the Middle Ages. Several are still in our language:* se mor-fondre *[to mope] dates from the twelfth century,* ver-moulu *[worm-eaten] from the thirteenth,* sau-poudré *[sprinkled] from the fourteenth,* boule-versé *[upset] from the fifteenth. The route that Felsen planned and followed was indeed vaulx-torte, starting with the first corner, the "hook" delineated on the map by Bondy, Le Bourget, and the Valenciennes road.*

I stopped, intuiting that Espopondie had something to add to this further reading of his gloss.

"We have almost reached the end of our labors," he said. "But you are right to stop. What is left is both the most difficult and the least important. I could have described the last step, although to a lesser degree, in the same manner. We obtained the meaning of the second line (step C) logically, but more laboriously than we reached the solution of the two puzzles 'forest of queens' and 'black monk' (step B). And this solution itself, although simple, was less immediate than digging out the first—and long-accepted—obvious facts: 'by night,' 'in gray,' 'will come within Varennes,' and the entire fourth line (step A). In short, we have gone from things that are clear to things that are less clear, which is as it should be. I still believe that the interpretation as a whole (A, B, C) is probable, but the importance of the results has dwindled at the same time as the complexity of the process has increased. If you do not accept my analysis of the second line (C), it will remain mysterious but will not constitute an objection to the results of the first steps (A and B). For almost four centuries no other acceptable explanation has been set forth, and a rather large portion of the quatrain will still be legible, with the future prisoner of the Temple dressed in gray going by night into Varennes after having passed through the forest that was deadly for queens, then, with the power created by elections, unleashing the violent events that will end up with the blade. Now let us move on to step D and to this strange word *Herne,* with the thought that whether or not we manage to throw some credible light upon it, it too will be incapable of wrecking the exegesis of the remainder of the second line, and all the more incapable of destroying our analysis of the other three."

I started to read again:

One word remains mysterious. In France, at least, there is no mention of "Herne" as the name of a person or a place. Because it is also not a "common noun," we have only three approaches at our disposal: its position in the line; what we know about how certain proper nouns are treated in the Centuries; *and finally the structure of the word, the letters and syllables of this* hapax. *Is this enough to construct a proof? No. But, yes, perhaps enough to rough out a plausible hypothesis. In what follows, the verbs may be in the affirmative mode, but this is merely to simplify the style; only the hypothetical mode is appropriate.*

A preliminary reflection: the word is unnecessary, because the logical sequence of the line is complete without it. There are only "two parts" (a), and their two divergent itineraries, almost opposite at the beginning, are sufficiently indicated (b and c). "Herne" does not form a coherent whole with these two pieces of information; it forms by itself a sort of parenthesis within the parenthesis. Because "vaul-torte" and "the white rock" concern the places *of the two "parts," we must look toward the* persons *acting in these places to find the meaning of this capitalized word.*

Position: this apparently unnecessary word comes neither before nor after the two pieces of information concerning itinerary, but rather between them. It separates them. It functions, therefore, as a signpost at a junction, and the logical structure of the line can be summarized with a few signs:

N
↑
"two itineraries: └── *Herne* ⟶ *E"*

*Methods used by Nostradamus: although most of the proper nouns in the quatrains have their usual form, others are changed. First there are the amputations necessitated by prosody (*Carpen *for "Carpentras" in 5.76c) or abbreviations that are sometimes rather pronounced (*Orl. Roüan *for "Orléans, Rouen" in 4.61d, etc.). But there are also transformations of many different sorts, the reasons for which escape us: exact inversion (*Eiovas *for "Savoie"); the exchanging of two letters (*Rapis *for*

"Paris," Argel for "Alger," Loin for "Lyon"); and in other places major disruptions (Nersaf for "France," Norlaris for "Lorraine"). One of the most remarkable instances is Chiren (Chyren) for "Henri" ("Henry," properly "Henric"): the last and first letter are linked at the beginning of the word in the French ch; then comes the rest of the last syllable (ir or yr) reversed, and the new word ends with the remainder of the first syllable (en)—not reversed. The only conclusion we can draw from this brief survey is that the author of the Centuries saw himself as having every right to "name without naming" countries, cities, and characters, and that Herne may represent yet another sort of word invention.

Finally, the structure of the word: Herne contains all the letters that the two names, Fersen and Reine, have in common, and, with the exception of the initial silent h, contains only these letters. Moreover, in the first syllable, the one adjoining vaultorte, the order of the letters is the same as that found in (F)er(sen), and in the second syllable, which adjoins "the white rock," the order is the same as in (Rei)ne. Thus, when analyzed, Herne brings the "two parts" together and at the same time sets them in opposition, characterizing each part by the person who is—in sentimental rather than political terms—the principal actor: Fersen and his servant turn in the direction of Le Bourget and Belgium, and the queen and her family journey on toward the white countryside of Champagne.

Earlier, Childéric and Blitilde, the ghosts of Bondy forest, put the misfortune of the last royal couple before the Revolution into the realm of Aeschylus. Now, with this monogram, the queen and her devoted escort belong to our Racine. The made-up word Herne does more than unite them; it binds them together at the very moment that a horse and a carriage separated them. It is an admirable scene. Postilions in their saddles awaited the signal. Fersen moved away from the enormous coach and took his leave of Marie-Antoinette:

"Adieu, Madame Korff!"

That was the name on the queen's passport, the name of a Russian baroness who was a friend of the Swede. They would only see each other once again, seven months later and three evenings in a row, during a daring visit Fersen was able to make to the Tuileries that he mentions in *his journal. And then events gathered speed. On August 13, 1792, the journal expressed the best commentary on the final line of Nostradamus's quatrain, "élu cap cause tempête, feu, sang, tranche":*

> *Terrible news from Paris. Thursday morning the chateau was attacked, the king and queen saved in the Assembly. At one o'clock there was still fighting in the courtyards and the Carrousel. Blood flowed, many killed, many hanged, the chateau broken into all over, eight cannons trained on it and fired. Romainvilliers killed, Daffy as well; thick smoke made one think the chateau had been set on fire. My God, how awful!*

Mysterious carriers would continue to smuggle letters for a long time. Even after August 10. Even after January 21. In April 1793, stubbornly hopeful, Fersen still stipulated to the "august widow of the Temple," as Georges Lenôtre called her, the action she should take when the army led by Dumouriez entered Paris to proclaim her regent. Dumouriez, however, did not enter Paris and, on October 16, at eleven-thirty in the morning, Marie-Antoinette, erect and disheartened, her hands tied behind her back, went by in the wagon of those condemned to death, leaving David's eyes with the lines of her finest portrait.

Here the manuscript came to an end with a new transcription of the quatrain with its logical punctuation:

> *By night will come through the forest of queens*
> *—Two parts: vaultorte (Herne) the white rock—*
> *The black monk in gray within Varennes.*
> *Elected head causes tempest, fire, blood, blade.*

At this moment Espopondie, who had listened to my reading as attentively as did his friends, as if discovering his text, gestured to me to put down the bundle of papers.

"I wrote, I think, a few more pages of reflections, but I would prefer to hear yours. Because you do me the favor of frequently coming to see me, you will be able to tell me what you think is weak, excessive, or tendentious in these old analyses. If the essential survives the blades and saws of your criticism, we in turn will construct a philosophical coach in which we all are coachmen. We'll see just where it takes us . . . But I forgot! A few years after writing these notes I went back to the *Centuries*, to some other quatrains. In my papers there must be some little document of what I found."

He turned to me. "Tomorrow we'll start looking for that. Too bad that all these musings weren't put away side by side, but you know all the little storerooms we make for our ideas as well as for our love life. Squirrels have more than one larder and the saints' bones several reliquaries."

Because it was late at night our friends left quickly, promising to return with their reflections and criticism. Espopondie and I ate a light supper and I took my leave without there being any question tonight of our playing Vulcan.

3

When I arrived the next day, Espopondie told me that he had a clearer memory now. There was no other bundle of paper, but at most a page of notes that would probably have been stuck into his copy of the *Centuries* at the page where the thirty-fourth quatrain of century 9 was to be found. Even if the quatrains seem to be distributed as the result of protracted and perhaps numerous shufflings, like cards that have been honestly prepared, there are sometimes two or three relating to one and the same portent that end up relatively close to each other in the book. This, we may be confident, is the case with 9.20 and 9.34.

"The reason I didn't write anything about 9.34," he went on, "is that, as far as the essentials are concerned, except for the fourth line, I would have had nothing to change from what is already found in the usual commentaries. The abundance of proper nouns in these lines has provided a guide and a preventive, safeguarding interpretation. Perhaps, before introducing our friends to what I had written about the first quatrain, I would have done well to let them take a look at the second, which names in one and the same phrase, in plain language, the count of Narbonne and Sauce, the grocer."

I went immediately to the third bookcase to get the *Centuries*. The page was right there. There were only a few words on it:

> *See Le Pelletier, but:*
>
> *In line a:* le part *is* le départ *[the departure], contrasted with* retour *[return] in line b;* solux*: Latin* solutus *(and not* solus*!);* mary *is husband (*mari, *not* marri *[afflicted]!), cf. 10.55c;*
>
> *Line b:* conflict *in the sense of "battle," a dozen examples;*
>
> *Line d: should we read* par conte *(= compte [account])* aux (s)avons d'huile*? Cf. 3.78b.*
>
> *The punctuation is obviously wrong in all four lines, mechanically reduced, as so often, to a single break after the second line.*
>
> *For the rest, Le Pelletier is fine*

I read the quatrain, or reread it, for it is just as well known as the first. Espopondie had written in the quite probable punctuation suggested by Le Pelletier and completed it in his copy.

> *Le part soluz (mary sera mitré),*
> *Retour. Conflict passera sur le thuille*
> *Par cinq cens. Un trahyr sera tiltré*
> *Narbon et Saulce par *couteaux *avons d'huille.* *

* The differences between one of the standard English translations of this quatrain and one that conforms more closely to what Dumézil and his friends decide the words mean may be of interest. The standard English translations have frequently diverged slightly, but in this case these differences are substantial:

> The separated husband shall wear a miter,
> Returning, battle, he shall go over the tiles,
> By five hundred, one dignified shall be betrayed,
> Narbon and Saulce shall have oil by Quintal.
> (Roberts, *Complete Prophecies of Nostradamus*)
>
> The lone part (husband shall wear a miter),
> Return. Battle will pass over the tile
> By five hundred. One traitor will be titled
> Narbon and Saulce by knives have oil.
> (My translation)

[Trans.]

"The two sentences from *Conflict* to *Saulce* are clear," Espopondie said. "*Conflict* in the *Centuries* is a frequent synonym for 'war' in the political and diplomatic sense, but also a synonym for 'battle,' with its physical violence. The word fits with what took place—the rifles and cannons at the Tuileries during the riots of 1792. Look at Le Pelletier's notes."

I read:

> (Concerning *le thuille* [the tile]) *Le Thuille*, the Palace of the Tuileries, begun in 1564 by Catherine de Médicis at the site of old tile kilns and completed under Louis XIV. This palace did not exist during the lifetime of Nostradamus. It became the sovereign's residence only under Louis XV.
>
> (Concerning *cinq cens* [five hundred]) These are the five hundred federated citizens of Marseilles who marched at the head of the Parisian rebels during the night of August 9 and 10, 1792, the decisive moment in the fall of the monarchy of Louis XVI. In l'*Histoire de la Révolution française* by A. Thiers (vol. 2, chap. 4, 209), one reads: "The Committee of the Insurrection (headquartered in the Jacobin convent) came to an understanding with Barbaroux, who promised the cooperation of the Marseillais, whose arrival was impatiently awaited . . . The firm and final plan was that they would assemble as an armed force at the chateau and depose the king." (Ibid., chap. 5, 235): "Finally on June 30 the Marseillais arrived. There were five hundred of them . . . Barbaroux went at their head to Charenton." (Ibid., 257): "Insurrection was proclaimed. It was then eleven-thirty. The Marseillais formed at the *porte des Cordeliers* and seized some cannons, their numbers swelling with the addition of a large crowd that lined up at their sides." (Ibid., 266): "The Marseillais marched at the head of the columns with the federated Bretons and they trained their weapons on the chateau."

Espopondie stopped me. "Yes, with those two details about place and number, the sentence concerning the conflict of the 'Thuille' can hardly mean anything else. Even the verb is well chosen: the five hundred Marseillais did not set themselves up in either the buildings or the courtyards of the chateau; their attack 'passed' over it, like an army corps across a battlefield. Now look at the final sentence. It denounces the 'betrayal' of an individual 'entitled Narbon[ne].' Now, there was only one 'Narbonne' who played an important role in French politics, and he did so just at this moment in history. Louis, the bastard son of Louis XV, although supposedly the son of an obliging gentleman, the count of Narbonne, was in fact the minister of war for Louis XVI during the winter of 1791–92. But, one 'betrayal' requiring another, Narbonne is joined on the pillory by Sauce, the grocer who, unfortunately for him, replaced the syndic of Varennes on the night that Louis XVI 'came within.'"

I still remembered well my history of the French Revolution and the names of these two individuals.

"Traitors to whom, traitors or not, it's not for us to decide," Espopondie went on. "But the fact is that both managed to get themselves accused of treason by royalists as well as republicans. The plan thought up by Narbonne to reinvigorate the monarchy thwarted the queen's plan and earned him simultaneously the hostility of the chateau, the hatred of his fellow ministers, and the mistrust of the Assembly. Sauce, the grocer, no doubt sincerely wished to shelter the royal family by welcoming it into his shack, but the result was that he prevented its escape. Nonetheless, he too, after a few days of enthusiasm and popularity, would encounter only jealousy and increasing suspicion on the part of his compatriots, to the point that he had to leave Varennes for good."

"And the end of the last line?" I asked. "'Huile' [oil] certainly seems to be part of the stock of a grocery store, and I know that there were witnesses who saw the queen at Sauce's, sitting in the midst of bundles of candles. But there is nothing intelligible to be found in the words between Sauce's name and this detail about oil."

"Indeed. The text is certainly faulty, because the verb form *avons* [we have] makes no sense and *couteaux* doesn't make much more. Frequently in the *Centuries* there are words, 'little words,' especially, that have been poorly identified and poorly parsed by the editors. I remember—where was that?—the phrase 'l'on sacre à Saturne' [one crowns him at Saturn], present in the editions by both Rigauds; this obviously should be corrected to read 'consacré à Saturne' [consecrated to Saturn]. Elsewhere, *en tout* [in all] ought to be read *entour* [surroundings]; *tardue* has replaced *tard le* [late the]. In yet another place, in 'auprès du lac Trasimen l'axur prinse' [near Lake Trasimen (?)], the last two words are *la surpri[n]se* [the surprise], badly transcribed. Look at the text that this slip of paper refers to."

I turned to the seventy-eighth quatrain of century 3:

> *Le chef d'Escosse, avec six d'Allemagne*
> *Par gens de mer Orient aux captif,*
> *Traverseront le Calpre et Espagne.*
>
> (The head of Scotland, with six from Germany
> By sea people Orient to the captive,
> Will traverse Calpre and Spain.)

That is the absurd text found in the first edition, but in 1568 it was corrected to "Par gens de mer Orientaux captif," that is, made prisoner by Oriental sailors.

"In our quatrain," Espopondie went on, "the opposite probably took place and the 1568 edition did not correct it. An independent *aux* must have been combined with the substantive preceding it. Because we are on the premises of an oil merchant, *savons* [soaps] are not unexpected. Therefore, I think we have to restore the end of the last line as *aux savons d'huile* [with soaps of oil]—a rather nice periphrasis for the 'candles' that spent a long time in close proximity to Marie-Antoinette. There is no doubt that these *savons* are hidden in the impossible *avons*. When the end of this line was altered, the initial *s* of *savons* must have merged with the *x* in *aux*. From time to time in the *Centuries*, an initial consonant will be dropped in the same manner. Thus, somewhere in the final quatrains of century 8 we find 'Par Arnani Tholoser isle franque' [Through Arnani Tholoser French island], with *isle* corrected in the 1568 edition to *ville* [city]; most likely the *v* of *ville* had been misunderstood and was transformed into *r*—the strange ending found on the name Toulouse—'Tholose[r].'

"As for the substantive to which *aux* is attached here, it cannot be *coût* [cost], which would have been written *coust* according to Nostradamus's spelling system. Rather it is a misreading of *conte*, which is the equivalent of *compte* [account]. More than once in the *Centuries u* and *n* are thus interchanged. I'm not claiming that my results are brilliant, but the line is no longer unintelligible and it corresponds from beginning to end with Sauce's profession: 'Et Saulce, par compte aux savons d'huile' [And Sauce, by the account of the oil soaps].

"Moreover, *compte* fits in not only with the unfortunate shopkeeper's profession but also with the type of problem—the suspicion of treason—that his conduct toward the king would soon earn him, which explains the preposition *par*: the accounts would have been the means or the proof of 'betrayal.' The accounts, in fact, played an important role. Try to find Lenôtre's book *Le drame de Varennes* (The Drama of Varennes), and look at the chapter entitled 'Le père Sauce.' I remember there being something about it."

I had no trouble locating the book and the passage. I read:

> Recriminations began the next day. They found it odd that the procurer-syndic had thus "seized the king in his house" for an entire night; there were many who were convinced that Louis XVI "had made [his host's] fortune" so that he would help him escape and that Sauce, the money in his possession, had kept the royal family locked up until the Parisian commissioners arrived; this was a double-edged accusation that incensed the patriots as much as the royalists. Others held him responsible for the reprisals that threatened Varennes, the expenses and nuisances of every sort that had been caused by the affair . . .
>
> . . . Although the mail daily brought congratulatory messages in which the name of Sauce was praised to the skies and extolled, elevated to the rank of the purest heroes of antiquity, the poor grocer-candlemaker found himself criticized, discredited, and reviled by his compatriots. One day he went to the municipality to make an honest declaration that upon examining his accounts he had come to discover a double entry of fifty pounds. He returned the amount to the secretary of the commune. Immediately he was ac-

> cused of embezzlement. Meetings were held "to bring him to judgment . . ." His enemies were unrelenting. His functions as procurer-syndic were taken away and he was reduced to the humble job of clerk to the justice of the peace. They went over his accounts with a fine-tooth comb and found some errors in them; they asked the department for authorization to prosecute him for the restitution of the money that he had no right to collect and to challenge the receipts provided. Obliged to leave Varennes, he emigrated to Saint-Mihiel, where he obtained work as clerk of the court.

"You see the importance of the accounts," Espopondie concluded, "in the unfortunately political career of this candle (according to the history) or oil-soap (according to the quatrain) merchant. The other quatrain—and this one too, in fact—showed us how Nostradamus sometimes deletes time, anticipating the result in the cause. This may be what is going on here: 'et Sauce par compte aux savons d'huile' would mean 'and Sauce, the merchant of candles, who, after the king's visit, will be accused, convicted of treason *by* his accounts.'"

"All right," I said. "But still the first line remains thorny."

"Not all that thorny. *Part,* in the masculine, can only be the substantive verb *partir* in its usual sense [to leave]; similarly, the *Centuries* uses the word *la pille,* derived from *piller* [to pillage], in the sense of booty. *Le part* is *le départ* [the departure]. In fact, *despart* in Nostradamus means something else—division or separation—which is connected to the other meaning of *partir,* a meaning that had disappeared before the sixteenth century but returns to the feminine substantive *la part.* Furthermore, Nostradamus is perfectly happy to strip the prefixes from compound words of this sort (*piation* for *expiation* [expiation], *viendra* for *deviendra* [will become], *porte* for *comporte* [consists of] . . .). *Le part* is therefore the exact opposite of *retour* at the beginning of the next line. It seems to form here a sort of ablative absolute with the participle *soluz*—which, in the Middle Ages, would have been *sols* and *solu.* 'Le part soluz . . . retour' can be glossed using one of the meanings of the Latin verb *solvere,* to solve or to resolve (usually the only meaning of *soldre* in the Middle Ages). Thus, 'The question of departure having been solved (negatively, by its failure), it is the return.' Or, if we use the first, etymological sense of *solvere*, to dissolve, it can be read as: 'The departure having been, as we say, eliminated [*liquidé*], having vanished into thin air like Perrette's dream, it is the return.' In both instances, because the remainder of the quatrain refers to the results of the drama of Varennes and even, in the last line, with the name 'Sauce,' to the drama itself, this departure that came to an end or this vanished project for departure and this return are those that took place on June 21, 22, and 23, 1791."

"You account for the first two words of the first line, but what do you make of the three others, 'mary sera mitré'?"

"If the word *retour* forms the principal proposition, with 'le part soluz' as its subordinate, the words 'mary sera mitré' play no part in either one. Moreover, the presence of a legitimate verb, *sera* [will be], proves that they are, in fact, autonomous. Once more we find one of those parentheses that are so frequent in the *Centuries*. The parenthesis would change nothing in the quatrain's balance, no matter what it meant, or even if no plausible sense could be attributed to it. But this is not the case. It has a probable meaning, one tragic and trivial: 'the husband [*mari*] will wear a Phrygian cap on his head.' First of all, *mary* most likely means 'husband' rather than—as Le Pelletier assumed—'afflicted' [*marri*]. The word only appears one other time in Nostradamus (I must have made a note of it in the margin), and this is its meaning."

There was, in fact, a passage noted in the margin—10.55. I turned to it and read:

Les malheureuses nopces celebreront
En grande ioye mais la fin malheureuse,
Mary et mere nore (= la bru) desdaigneront.

(They will celebrate the unhappy wedding
In great joy but the unhappy end
Husband and black mother [?] [= the daughter-in-law]
they will disdain.)

"As for *mitré*," Espopondie went on, "the word has, for a long time, been interpreted on the basis of the Latin *mitra*, the bonnet that the Phrygians of the Near East wore before it became the bishops' miter. Look and see if there is not a note about it in Le Pelletier."

I read:

> The so-called bonnet of liberty recalls the ancient headdress of the priests of Mithras [*sic*!] by its Phrygian shape. In Thiers's history of the Revolution, there is an account of the events of June 20, 1792 (vol. 2, chap. 3, 152): "The chateau (of the Tuileries) was evacuated (by the populace that had taken it by force). The crowd withdrew peacefully and in an orderly manner. It was about seven o'clock at night. Immediately the king, the queen, her sister, and her children came together, all weeping copiously. The king, dazed by this scene, was still wearing the red bonnet on his head. Noticing it for the first time in several hours, he threw it down indignantly."

"That's the one. You'll notice that the king is no more directly designated here than in quatrain 20. 'The black monk' who came within Varennes through the forest of queens is here *le mary* [the husband], in another reference to the person closely linked to him and the one who, more than he, was calling the tune in this adventure in which they both would lose—the queen. Moreover, once again the order of the scenes interjects the consequence (in the future) into the cause: 'after the failure of the departure—and the consequence of this failure will be the symbolic bonnet rammed onto the king's head—it is the return.'"

"This question of order seems to me important," I said.

"Yes, we shall consider that with our friends. It is probably a characteristic of thought expressed in quatrains. Besides, if you compare quatrain 20 as a whole with quatrain 34, you can already remark something about the order in both. The first three lines of the first describe episodes in their actual order, with the exception of the premonition, implied in the words 'black monk,' while he is still in the carriage, of the king's imprisonment in the Temple. Those are closely spaced episodes that took place one after the other in less than twenty-four hours: the stopover at Bondy, the divergent routes taken by Fersen and the berline, the arrival at Varennes. Then, between the third and fourth lines something like an abyss opens up. On top of a number of other episodes left unmentioned, there are suddenly enumerated the final and most dramatic consequences, leaving a void several seasons long between the arrival at Varennes and the deposition and finally the death of the king. But it is this void, on the contrary, that quatrain 34 marks out in broad strokes. Putting off until later the 'elected head' and the tempestuous events this head provokes in 20d, 34a picks up the thread of events just after the inopportune arrival in Varennes. After the failure of the departure it is the return.

"Here too, between 'the departure' and 'the return' a parenthesis plainly anticipates, in the Phrygian bonnet forced on the king, the first—and not yet bloody—violence that will result from this forced return after a lapse of a year, almost to the day: the first invasion of the Tuileries in June 1792. Then, as if the author had reflected upon what—or rather, who—was responsible for this worsening situation, we are taken back to the moment of real or supposed treason by the titled traitor, Narbonne, who, in fact, was in charge of the politics of the cabinet from December 6, 1791, to March 10, 1792. Finally, one traitor recalls another, and we are thrown further into the past, to the fatal night of June 21–22, 1791, to Sauce, the syndic of Varennes. We have just looped the loop from the first to the last words of the quatrain: the misfortunes stemming from the grocer-candlemaker trace back to him and condemn him."

"That is all logical, but its logic is dreadfully flexible!"

"Agile rather than flexible. Thought runs from one episode to another like a pianist's fingers on the keys. Sometimes it creates harmonies and vague reminders. The events as they emerge from the quatrains make a melody."

"Is it sound to construct theory on the basis of two quatrains that constitute only a single piece of evidence? To describe the methods of thought behind them one would have to have analyzed and interpreted a great many . . ."

"Not necessarily. The analytic laboratory is provided with extensive material by the dense detail in this pair of quatrains."

"Still, some other examples would be welcome. Don't you know any others? Why did you never develop your Nostradamian philology?"

"There is at least one quatrain from among those relating to Napoleon that is impressive because of the periphrasis that seems to comment on history's 'little shaven-head' and because of the precise information about the duration of a reign that was 'tyrannical,' in the Greek sense—that is, not resulting from any hereditary legitimacy, but usurped or conquered."

Quickly I located one of the three quatrains in which "close-cropped head" or "shaven head" is mentioned (7.13) and read it:

De la cité marine et tributaire
La teste rase prendra la satrapie:
Chasser sordide qui puis sera contraire;
Par quatorze ans tiendra la tyrannie.

(From the maritime and tributary city
The close-cropped head will assume satrapy:
Dismiss the vile who then oppose him;
For fourteen years hold tyranny.)

Then I improvised its gloss just for fun:

"Leaving Ajaccio, on the island only recently acquired, the future 'Little Shaven-head' will elevate himself to supreme power and will chase out the corrupt individuals who later will oppose him. He will hold the empire for fourteen years."

"Hm! He might be coming from his Corsican town or beginning his glorious career by making Toulon surrender, he might be chasing out the vile Directory or the detested Englishman or simply dismissing Talleyrand, because all these things have been suggested . . ."

"I see. Your requirement is that a quatrain contain at least a rare proper name or its equivalent before you give it your careful attention."

"Yes. The 'Cropped Head' is perhaps as good as a proper name . . ."

That is where we stopped. Espopondie was visibly tired. After the light supper that was our usual routine I suggested that, this evening once again, we give up on exploring and burning the personal past of the master of the house. As I was taking my leave he said, "If you have time, go over the philological framework of this old demonstration and complete it. Treat Nostradamus like a serious author. Make a glossary of his words. Explain him through himself. It is more reliable than emptying dictionaries of old French onto his quatrains. In three days you will reread or summarize my text for our young friends and we shall hear what they have to say about it."

4

I spent the next two mornings and a portion of my days working on Nostradamus as if he were Virgil and on Espopondie's glosses as if Servius, the grammarian, had written them. I found nothing to weaken Espopondie's thesis. All I could do was accumulate further parallel examples for each instance he had examined. These are dull lists, and there is no harm if readers prefer to skip them, returning to them later should they become caught up in the game.

I began with quatrain 34. I had no trouble consolidating the corrections in spelling and breaks that Espopondie proposed in the unintelligible fourth line, correcting "et Saulce par coutaux avons d'huile" to "et Saulce par conte" (that is, *compte*) "aux savons d'huile."

As examples of words broken in the wrong place, in addition to the example our master had located (4.78b), I found the others he mentioned: "l'on sacre à Saturne" in 8.29a, "en tout" in 2.44a, and "l'axur prinse" in 6.39c. And I added, in 6.80b, "feu la cité et l'anne tranchera," in which the edition of 1568 had corrected *l'anne* to *lame* [blade] of a sword. *Coutaux* or *couteaux* substituted for *conte aux* merely presents an identical mistake where two words merge into one, as in the dreadful *tardue* of 2.96c, properly divided in the second Rigaud's edition as *tard le.*

The same mistaken *u* of that line *(cout[e]aux)*, which Espopondie had corrected to an *n*, can be found elsewhere. For example: *n* had become *u* in 6.34b, where *au* is *un* badly written, and the opposite substitution takes place in 9.51c, where the correct reading is *au* (1568) rather than *an* (1566).

In the first line of the same quatrain (6.34a), Espopondie read *le part* as the equivalent of *le départ*, and I found the parallels he had mentioned: *piation* in 9.46b, *viendra* in 1.88c, *porte* in 5.60b.

I spent more time working on several problems of meaning raised by quatrain 20, starting with the fourth line. I checked that Espopondie was correct in his brief justification of *cap[.]* as the equivalent of *chef* rather than the abbreviation of *Cap[et]*, and in his refusal to translate *esleu* (which has the quite precise meaning of "persons elected") as "constitutional," because, far from "electing" Louis XVI, the constitution limited itself to establishing that the Capetian dynasty ruled and merely asked the sixteenth Louis to accept certain limitations on his power.

In the first line I was astonished at the spelling of the word *Reines*. In 7.6a, 9.77c, and 10.17a, the word is *Royne* or *les Roynes*, which was the usual spelling in the mid-sixteenth century. Does the *ei* of *Reines* prefigure the pronunciation that was dominant in Paris much later? In any case its most natural sense here is as "regina." I no longer know who had the nerve to correct *Reines* to "Reims," on the pretext that the berline had encountered the "forest of Reims" along its route. And what about the rhyme?

In the second line I did not spend much time over "deux pars," because the sense of *part (pars)* meaning *partie (parties)* (or *parti*) is the usual one in *Centuries*, and not just in the expression "la plus part" (2.57c and 83b, 6.61b) or "la plus grand part" (3.59b, 4.35b, 6.13b), but in general. Thus in 3.99c, we read "Camps de deux parts conflict sera si aigre" [Camps of two parts battle will be so bitter], and in 4.80b "en quinze pars sera l'eau divisée" [into fifteen parts the water will be divided]. The occupants of the berline in 1791 would also be separated—disastrously—into "deux pars." There is no basis in Nostradamus for reading "deux pars" as the two elements of a married couple.

Vaultorte took up most of my time. The word was obviously formed as Espopondie had said. Making two lists, I amused myself by expanding and comparing the lines in which the preposition logically introducing the complement is present and the lines in which it has been left out. It seems that Nostradamus used both constructions indiscriminately.

Present (particularly true of the various values of the preposition *par*):

> *3.91a–b: L'arbre qu'était* par *long tems mort séché*
> Dans *une nuit viendra a reverdir.*
> (The tree that was *for* a long time dead dry
> *In* one night shall grow green again.)
> *8.19c:* De *mort famille sera presque accablee.*
> (*By* death family will be almost overwhelmed.)
> *8.59d:* par *mer chassé*
> (pursued *by* sea)
> *8.75c: La mère à Tours* du *fils ventre aura enfle.*
> (At Tours the mother will have her belly swollen *by* the son.)
> *9.9c: eau passant* par *crible*
> (water running *through* a sieve)
> *9.97d: premiers* en *brèche entrez, etc.*
> (first ones enter *into* the breach, etc.)

Left out:

> *3.17a: Mont Aventine brusler nuit sera veu* (= pendant *la nuit).*
> (Mount Aventine will be seen to burn night [= *during* the night].)
> *6.89b: de miel face oint (*= sur *la face)*
> (with honey face ointment [= *on* the face])
> *8.8d: Dedans Turin rapt épouse emmener (*par *rapt), etc.*
> (Within Turin rape wife to lead [= *by* rape], etc.)

Then, finally, I gave some thought—or reverie—to the final proposition, the *Herne* in the second line. I had nothing to add, and the initial *H* instead of *F*, which seemed to require explanation, continued to bother me.

The reader should not worry; that is the end of this philology. The next two evenings Espopondie and I, silently agreeing to set Nostradamus aside, went back to our daily task. A great many papers were thrown into the fire with very little comment.

The third evening our two friends, de Momordy and Charles Leslucas, arrived right on time. By five o'clock the "society of thought," as we called it then, was fully assembled. Espopondie asked me to read quatrain 34 and then, to refresh our memories, to give a brief summary of his paper concerning quatrain 20. I did that, emphasizing the links, the varying degrees of obviousness or likelihood—A, B, C, D—and using my own statistics when the opportunity arose. It was after seven by the time I had finished, too late for any discussion; besides which, our two friends requested that we postpone this so that they might develop their ideas. Both of them, moreover, were well acquainted with these passages in the *Centuries*, quatrain 34 as well as quatrain 20; who among us had not been curious about Nostradamus during adolescence? They thought Espopondie's arguments were well constructed but they wanted to go back to the book itself and study its philology critically, verifying the bits of history marshaled at Bondy and the Temple and in the "tempest" of 1792.

When we met again several days later they had indeed done some work. De Momordy, although complimenting Espopondie for his wisdom, was the first to say he had come up against a few difficulties.

He had consulted the list of communes in France, in which he had found that Varennes is a very ordinary place name. Departments from Aisne to Tarn-et-Garonne, from Maine-et-Loire to Côte-d'Or, contained no fewer than thirty-one, of which seven were hamlets: twelve Varennes, one Les Varennes, five Varennes with some other name (such as Varennes-Changy), one Varennes-le-Grand, and the rest with prepositions (Varennes sur, sous, lès, en, such as Varennes-sur-Loire and Varennes-lès-Mâcon). Did not such an abundance diminish the singularity of the place named only once in the *Centuries*?

I answered that in my opinion Espopondie had anticipated the objection. The only Varennes mentioned in history is Varennes-en-Argonne; no other has a nocturnal arrival worthy of inscription, and no other has any particular connection with a bloody political crisis such as the one linked by the last line of quatrain 20 to the three preceding lines. Nor does the approach to any one of them entail mentioning "white rock."

On the other hand, de Momordy was well acquainted with the fact that, following their execution, the Knights Templars' inheritance, and particularly the Temple, had been given to the Hospitalers of Saint Jean of Jerusalem by the greedy Philip the Fair. He received, in return, a substantial sum of money, even though it had been given to them for free by papal bull in 1312, in accordance with a decision by the Council of Vienna. But were they still there when the Revolution nationalized the possessions of the clergy and got rid of the Temple, a temple that moreover had been rebuilt and was quite different from the original fortress? Besides, at the end of the eighteenth or even the sixteenth century, were the Hospitalers really the "black monks" that they earlier had been because of their Benedictine heritage and, in contrast to the Knights
Templar, the easily offended possessors of the color white?

I was able to reassure de Momordy on both these points. I would have expected him to be better informed, although of course his nobility had been awarded by the judiciary. I only had to go to the next room to find the last part of the seven-volume Larousse dating from the beginning of the century—this being the one we still regularly used in 1924. There he could read at the word *Temple*:

> The monastery had been established in the second half of the twelfth century, northeast of the city outside the walls of Philip Augustus. The Knights Templar were succeeded by the Hospitalers of Saint Jean of Jerusalem, who set up the great priory of France there. It remained thus privileged, less and less a fortress and more and more a palace, and its last important alterations date from less than twenty years prior to the Revolution. Louis XVI and the royal family were imprisoned there following the riots of August 10, 1792. After having sheltered other famous prisoners—an Eng-

> lish admiral, Pichegru, Moreau, Cadoudal—it was torn down in 1811 and immediately replaced with a building in the style of Les Halles. At the beginning of our century this structure was in turn assigned to the pickax in 1904.

As for the color of their robes, I turned to another volume and had him skim through the article "Malta (Order of)." The order of the Hospitalers of Saint Jean of Jerusalem was founded in 1099, and its rule was permeated with Benedictine ideals. The rule received the confirmation of Pope Pascal II, and in 1130, Innocent III transformed the order, making the armed defense of Christians against the infidels its most important duty. After Jerusalem fell to Saladin in 1191, the Hospitalers based themselves at Acre, where they remained for an entire century. They then moved to Cyprus, and then to Rhodes, which they had just conquered (1320). From then on they were called "The Order of the Knights of Rhodes." They won great fame in their defense of the island against Mahomet II in 1480, but in 1522, after six months of magnificently defending themselves, they had to surrender honorably to Suleiman II. They were once again transformed in 1530 after Charles V set them up on the island of Malta. They took the name "Knights of Malta," which survived, with all its prestige, until our day. The order, when established, was made up of three classes: nobles or knights, priests or chaplains, and the lay brothers who assisted both groups. As for the costume—the essential element—I myself finished reading:

> The correct habit consisted of a black robe with a peaked cloak; in wartime it included a red coat of arms. In addition, on the left side of his breast, every knight wore a cross of white cloth with four arms of equal length extending from the center to the edge and forming eight points as a sign of the beatitudes to which he should aspire.

For the benefit of de Momordy, I added ironically that, in the *Malet*, the manual that taught me the history of the Middle Ages when I was a seventh grader at Neufchâteau, I had learned—and retained—that there were or had been three orders of soldier-monks:

the Knights of Saint Jean of Jerusalem, the Knights of the Temple, and, in the north, the Teutonic Knights. The *Malet* also said that these orders, the first two of which formed a sort of permanent army in Palestine, revealed their double character, religious and military, in their very costume: they wore a knight's armor but with a monk's robe underneath. For the Hospitalers, the robe was black with a white cross on the breast; for the Knights Templar it was white with a red cross. The Order of Malta remained faithful to its origins with its black robe: black were the inhabitants of the Temple in Nostradamus's time, and the monks who served the great priory until November 2, 1789, were still black.

Charles Leslucas then picked up where de Momordy left off. At first it was to administer a soothing balm to the most delicate point in the paper, the fourth word of the second line of the twentieth quatrain: *Herne*. He found the idea of a sentimental monogram ingenious: what couple has not traced on a wall or carved into bark a certificate of their union? They should scrape the phantoms from the trees of a hundred and forty years ago on the grounds at Versailles . . . As for the *H* in *Herne*, he reminded us that there was a similar example both in the most modern French and in the French used by Nostradamus: the Latin word *foris* 'outside of' had in the normal course of events produced *fors* [except], so that François I, following his defeat and imprisonment at Pavie, was able to say that "all is lost, save honor *[fors l'honneur]*." But very early, beginning in the eleventh century, a rival to this legitimate heir appeared, an intruder that has virtually replaced it in our usage: *hors*. "The spectator forgives all," said Voltaire, echoing the words of the captive Valois king, "except *[hors]* languor." The same thing happened with both simple and compound words, so that we see *hormis* [save for] and *dehors* [outside] alongside *forclore* [to exclude], and *forfaire* [to be false] and *hors-la-loi* [outlaw] next to *forcené* [fanatic].

Charles Leslucas added that Nostradamus frequently traveled in the south of France, where there were also many Spaniards on the move, sniffing out our civil wars and armed with Charles V's still-recent prestige. Now, had not all the initial *f*s in Latin become *h*s in

Spanish? Where the French say *fils* [son], the Spanish say *hijo*; *faire* [to make or do] is *hacer* in Spanish . . . Under these conditions, and because this quatrain seems to abound in puzzling expressions that are intended to suggest something without saying it, to reveal while hiding, may we not think that the transformation of *F* into *H* had suggested itself to Nostradamus or his mysterious inspirer as a way to designate Fersen without disclosing him?

But Charles Leslucas had a problem somewhere else. Was it really in the forest of Bondy that Childéric II and his wife, Blitilde, had been assassinated? He thought that he had read somewhere that it was in the forest of Chelles.

Espopondie, who had been listening absentmindedly, spoke up. "Yes, there is some uncertainty about it, really without importance. You should find a note card at the end of my paper."

I found it and read:

According to pseudo-Frédégaire, the only chronicler who has provided us with information, the double murder took place in "Lauconis Silva." This name, "Lauco[n-]," has left no direct trace on the toponymy: it should be something more or less like "Laon," because the city of Laon is the former Laudunum. Most of the old historians, as well as the modern ones who have annotated the chronicle, understand it as the forest of Bondy or of Livry, which comes down to the same thing. But perhaps this is about a different spot nearby in the wooded plateau that in the early Middle Ages occupied the eastern arc of the belt around Paris. In 1867, Alfred Maury wrote in his Forêts de la Gaule *(although unfortunately without noting his sources):*

> *Along the right bank of the Seine, from Melun to Paris, there stretched a large forested band, divided early into three great forests:* sylva Vilcenna *(Vincennes),* Bungiacensis sylva *(Bondy), and* Liberiacensis sylva *(Livry). These three forests were all designated together, at the time that they formed a single entity, as* Lauchonia sylva. *That is where Childéric II was assassinated in 673 by Bodillon. After the forest was carved up the name "Lauchonia" disappeared, but the divisions were still extremely large forests.*

In fact, the name has not vanished. Abbé Lebeuf, well before Maury, had pointed out that "Lauconia" survived, no doubt, in the name "Lognes," a place located a half-league to the south of the Marne, opposite Chelles. In the seventh century, as Maury says, the forest was continuous from Bondy (and beyond) to the north down to Lognes (and beyond) to the south, and it encompassed Chelles (Calavilla regia), *which was the little Versailles or Rambouillet of the Merovingian kings. Now, for better or for worse, and without even mentioning the bloody ghost of Blitilde, all of the plateau certainly deserved the name "forest of queens." It was at Chelles that Childéric was assassinated by the mayor of the palace, who was the lover of the cynical queen Frédégonde. Also, erected near Chelles was the abbey founded in the sixth century by Clotilde and rebuilt in the seventh by Bathilde—the mother of our Childéric—and it was governed many times by abbesses of royal blood before it was finally destroyed in the "tempest" of 1791.*

This distraction had tired Espopondie, or perhaps, because none of it changed any part of his demonstration, it all seemed pointless.

"My friends," he said, "that's enough for tonight. In three days we shall really have to get down to the essentials."

Our friends left. During our evening meal Espopondie talked to me about something entirely different. His memory was full of spectacles and adventures from the Far East. Sometimes I felt I was hearing his friend the doctor, Paul-Louis Couchoud, who, a few months earlier, in his lavish villa, "La Muette," had recited—the way any good actor would—selections from *Sages et poètes d'Asie*.

5

Three days later we were rejoined by our friends, each of whom brought along his *Nostradamus*. Espopondie began to speak right away, seeming to have forgotten for the time being the risk he ran night and day with his heart, whose symptoms were all too clear to him.

"Let us acknowledge," he said, "that the converging data we have assembled confirm and even make compelling what the first and most immediately clear bits of information have suggested to commentators for almost a century and a half. We must, indeed, recognize the 'flight to Varennes' in quatrain 9.20. This great turning point in history has indeed been set before our eyes by Nostradamus. How awkward for us! The problems that result!

"Our first task, I believe, before we devote any thought to how it originated, is to define as closely as possible the characteristics of this unusual form of knowledge as it is fixed in the document.

"First, one is struck by the concentration, in the middle of the quatrain (the end of line b and the beginning of line c), of color notations: white earth, black monk in gray. It is as if Nostradamus were describing a picture, or rather a film, passing before his eyes. But this impression is deceptive. 'White' and 'gray' correspond to real things, one geographical and the other historical; Champagne is, in fact, white and the king was, in fact, disguised in gray. But 'black?' The king never was 'the black monk'; he was simply held captive in the Temple, which, until 1789, had belonged to monks who were recognizable by their black robes, in contrast to the white robes of the Knights Templar. Whence the most remarkable characteristic of the quatrain: despite the notations, all of which are concrete, onomastic, or descriptive, it is above all intellectual, considered, simultaneously synthetic and analytic.

"In the *present*: all that it retains (in a) and develops (in b) of the itinerary is the actual starting point and the decisive moment. Everything else is the disastrous consequence of these: the 'splitting' at Bondy that separates the royal family from its mentor, Fersen, and turns the king over to his bad hunch concerning Sainte-Menehould. In the distant *past*: the place where they were fatally separated evokes a particular foreboding tone from a thousand years earlier; it compares the exhaustion of both dynasties, Merovingian and Capetian, and the tragic ends of two royal couples, not simply the king but the king and queen jointly. In the *near future*: obliged to return from Varennes, the king found himself caught up in the rapid linkage of causes and effects that would bring him to the Temple (in c). Finally, in a *slightly more distant future*: the tyrannical Convention, the bloody events of 1792 and 1793, and the blade itself will be the logical outcome of the drama begun at Varennes (in d).

"But you can see that, throughout these intellectual processes inscribed in the quatrain's structure, one must distinguish not only the four chronological frameworks that I have just listed, but also the sorts of thought that occur with each. The connection between Varennes and 1793 is a simple statement, a sort of historical interpretation, as is the connection between Varennes and the Temple, in a certain sense. The 'black monk,' however, placed as he is in the carriage that has not yet deposited him at Varennes, is anachronistically anticipatory, if one may say so: the king will not be a 'black monk' until after Varennes. Nostradamus, or his 'source,' has therefore included the declaration of the consequence in the description of the cause, as if the visions and deductions had been crushed and mixed together at the brain's exit, and then had broken through the hole in disorder—at least in an outward disorder, because the 'black monk' and the disguise 'in gray' are combined, creating a striking contrast that is all the more interesting because it is not real and could not have been *seen*. It is, therefore, *constructed* by a somewhat literary artifice on the basis of a fact (the disguise in gray) and a metaphor (the assimilation of the king to his predecessors in the Temple, the black monks). This artifice suggests, by shifting the designation from 'gray' to 'black,' that the individual who 'shall come within Varennes' is not what he appears to be, but that there is a distortion, that he wears a disguise.

"'The forest of queens' presents an even more remarkable case. Elicited by the location of the first relay station in the 1791 flight, the connection between the ends met by both Blitilde and Marie-Antoinette, 'the queens,' is a pure construction that is simultaneously intellectual and aesthetic, full of philosophical and dramatic powers. This connection also is not part of the 'things seen.' All that could have been seen was the forest in which they separated, the relay post at Bondy whence Fersen departed on horseback toward the north while the other occupants of the berline headed east. The rest of the process is something that, in our mental practice, or rather in the vague jargon of psychologists, is called 'the association of ideas': one dynastic crisis evokes another that had been played out in the same place. Of course, as in any superposition of this sort, although the basic elements are in agreement, the details diverge. Louis XVI and Marie-Antoinette did not, like the Merovingian couple, die in the forest; what happened at Bondy, by depriving them of Fersen, was only the distant, delayed-action cause of the beheadings in 1793. It is nonetheless true that, in a 'lofty view' of history, reducing it to its main lines, the two dynasties' late leap toward the restoration of their power ended, and for similar reasons, in the two royal couples being put to death, one couple by feudal rebels, the other by a rebel third estate."

We were listening attentively to Espopondie without interrupting him when de Momordy remarked: "You have just said yourself, sir, that this paralleling of two murders committed a thousand years apart is a purely intellectual and aesthetic construction. It is, in fact, beautiful and poignant. But what makes you sure that it is not your own personal art or intelligence that, here at the beginning of the twentieth century, well informed and with some distance from the events of the seventh and eighth centuries, made this association of ideas and then projected it into a text where it fits well, in fact, but where it is not established?"

"My friend," Espopondie replied, "do you agree that the context, the second line, with the separation into the opposite paths of the 'two parts' historically made at Bondy, requires that we translate 'forest of queens' as 'forest of Bondy'?"

"I don't, in fact, see any other plausible explanation of the second line."

"Then, if the background comparison in the quatrain is not the one I am suggesting, how do you explain the plural 'queens'? The forested plateau that, I repeat, was established for us in the second line only deserves this royal periphrasis through the conjunction of two personal destinies, twin misfortunes, one there on the spot, the other in the long run, those of Blitilde and Marie-Antoinette. What other queens could this be about?"

"Sir, a truly ugly idea has occurred to me. What if Nostradamus was, after all, pulling a fast one and only spoke of the 'forêt de Reines' to rhyme with 'Varennes'? It would be a little like in Nerval's sonnet:

> Mon front est rouge encore du baiser de la reine,
> J'ai rêvé dans la grotte où nage la sirène.
>
> (My forehead is still red from the kiss of the queen,
> I have dreamt in the cave where the mermaid swims.)

It is clear that in 'Desdichado,' 'la reine' demanded 'la sirène,' unless the opposite is true and it would be pointless to try to identify the two with each other."

"From 'frênes' to 'lorraines,' there are plenty of perfect rhymes for 'Varennes.' Nostradamus would have had more than enough choices if he had let himself go, freely fantasizing. But that is not what is important. We must be faithful to our choice to take the *entire* quatrain seriously. Rhyme, of course, has its constraints and its temptations, and Nostradamus, far from wringing its neck, is always respectful of it, making it beautiful whenever possible. But what is distinctive about—I won't say poets, but even experienced versifiers—is that they *take advantage* of rhyme to say what they have to say elegantly and don't give in to it and say nothing."

Charles Leslucas spoke up. "You are right, sir, I think. But isn't it strange, even extreme, to locate an allusion to Marie-Antoinette in the plural 'queens,' where it would be thoroughly isolated, because the quatrain otherwise does not mention her?"

"You are forgetting the proper noun *Herne*, about which you yourself provided a small but interesting insight last week. But here we meet up with another characteristic of the mental mechanism now up for dissection in the twentieth quatrain. The case of the 'forest of queens' must not be separated from that of the 'black monk.' It is as if Nostradamus spoke in riddles so he would not reveal the august persons engaged in the adventure, most particularly, if you will allow me the expression, his 'lady,' or Fersen's 'lady,' in the chivalrous sense that the Middle Ages gave this title. In the entire quatrain the only things named without disguise are 'Varennes' and the indication of the time, 'shall come at night.' Everything else requires a translation."

It was de Momordy's turn to attack. "Despite the 'forest of queens,' where she is hidden in a plural as if behind a veil, and despite 'Herne,' where she has merged so well with her devoted escort that one can't tell where she begins or where she ends, admit that it is above all in your commentary that Marie-Antoinette is present."

"No, my friend," Espopondie replied. "It is in the event that took place in June 1791, where she is not only present but the most active person in the drama. Through the devotion she inspires in Fersen, through the influence she exerts on her husband, through her energy, all the honor and all the responsibility is hers:

> . . . behind a veil, invisible and present,
> She is of this quatrain the soul omnipotent,

and she is the one that Nostradamus, or his source—let's not make a choice between the hypotheses!—twice puts forward without revealing her face. Why? How can we know?"

"Perhaps I have an explanation," said Charles Leslucas. "The king and the queen are, in fact, glossed over in quatrain 20. And they are glossed over again at the beginning of quatrain 34, in which *départ* and *retour* have no expressed subject, or rather would have none if the parenthesis 'mari sera mitré' did not again recall enigmatically that this is about the departure and return of the king, and of the king both as king and as 'husband.' The result is that the queen this time is present again, but glossed over, glossed over to the second degree even, through the king, who is only mentioned himself through the relation he has with her. The faithful way in which Nostradamus customarily employs a protective cloud, like Homer's gods, is all the more remarkable because all the other characters, in quatrain 20 as well as in quatrain 34, are designated without any precautions or even named: the 'élu cap' is 'the head or the government resulting from elections' in the most technical sense of the phrase. And what about the two 'traitors' pilloried in 34 c and d—the 'entitled Narbon' and the unfortunate Saulce, with his oil soaps and his bookkeeping problems?"

"You are right," de Momordy conceded. "The name 'Narbon'—both because it is 'titled' and because it is paired with 'Saulce'—can only designate a man, the count of Narbonne, and not the city, although it too is sometimes shortened in the same way. The linking of the two proper nouns is easy and powerful: 'There will be someone who is titled who will betray (the king), (meaning) Narbon; and (there will be another with no title, meaning) Saulce . . .'"

"Thank you, my friend," said Charles Leslucas. "But what explains this difference in the treatment of the *minores*—thrust unceremoniously onto center stage—and that of the royal couple? Have you heard of this Viennese doctor who is beginning to have some disciples here, someone named Sigmund Freud? He has a simple, straightforward word for this sort of phenomenon: *censorship*. Nostradamus, or his source, conceals the king, whom he meets everywhere, and hides the queen's prominent role. Why? If I understand correctly what I am told about Freud, I think we may venture the following: Everything leads us to believe that Nostradamus, or his source, was a committed royalist and that, in the drama to come, he allied himself instinctively and vigorously with the royalists. That is why he—like the 'queen's party' at the Tuileries—described the action of the count of Narbonne as a 'betrayal,' even though historians are still undecided about his intentions. He was reproached for encouraging the war against Vienna, but perhaps he only did so to have at his disposal what Louis XVI had lacked in 1789 and 1791: an army capable of making the rebels see reason, as the army of Henri IV had done. So would it not be out of respect, reluctance, or scruple—whether conscious or unconscious—that he avoided presenting his idols by creating so many puzzles? One does not bring the Holy of Holies into the open."

"There must be something to that," said Espopondie. "We know enough about the close patron-protégé bonds that were established between the scholar-doctor-prophet and the royal family: Henri II, his widow Catherine, and his sons the kings. Let's follow this as far as it will take us. In all the future that he foresaw, let's say, or that was shown to him, the most dramatic moment, the moment above all that was most interesting and most loathsome, the moment with the most far-reaching consequences in both the near and the distant future, was the collapse of the monarchy. That, therefore, is where he focused most of his attention—on what for him was a catastrophe. He would have divided the history of France into 'two parts': before and after Varennes (1791), or at least before and after the Temple (1792) and the guillotine (1793). Moreover, it has long been noted that in the gobbledegook of the dedicatory epistle to Henri II, he noted the year 1792 as a 'revolutionary' date in the etymological sense of the word."

He turned toward me and said, "Look in the second volume of Le Pelletier. It comes a few pages before the end of the epistle."

I glanced through the epistle and found, straddling two pages, the long sentence predicting that a persecution of the Church, greater than the one carried out a thousand years earlier in Africa by the Vandals, "will last until the year one thousand seven hundred and ninety-two, which they will think to be a renovation of the century." Then I read Le Pelletier's note concerning the expression "renovation of the century," which smacks so strongly of Latin and plays with the concept of the secular: "That is *a new era*; the republican era dates, in fact, from September 22, 1792."

Caught up in the game, I took the liberty of glossing the sentence. "As far as the 'great persecution' forecast by this gibberish is concerned, the seer or his source could have seen it materialize three years before this fateful date, when the clergy's possessions were nationalized; but he could just as well have seen it begin earlier, in the eighteenth century's impiety, the Encyclopedists' undertaking, and the elimination of the Jesuits. At any rate, it was indeed in 1792 that this persecution culminated when the Church's final defense, the king's veto, vanished with the fall of 'Monsieur Veto' himself. In this sense, one can in fact say that as persecution specifically of the Church and limited to the Church, it would last 'until 1792,' later to vanish into the widespread horror, of which the sentencing of Louis XVI would be only the main symbolic episode. And this would be the case, Nostradamus says, as long as 'the Roman people' (by this we can understand: the Catholics) begin 'to recover and chase away some of the obscurity of darkness, getting some of their *[sic]* pristine brightness, not without great division and continual changes.' This, we can gather, will be the Concordat of 1804 and Chateaubriand's *Genius of Christianity*, as well as the entire tumultuous history of Catholicism in France after the brief Capetian restoration."

Espopondie met my comments with an encouraging smile and sent our examination off in another direction.

"Let's go back to where we started. It is as a painter that Nostradamus—no matter what his 'source' or inspiration—fixes certain details, primarily the colors of the second and third lines. But not everything is visual; otherwise we would have to think that his eyes lit on documents not yet written, and lingered there. Or perhaps they had seen Georges Lenôtre's erudite book, from which he could have borrowed names such as Sauce, even seeing Narbonne, perhaps, or Varennes. Would this not be one more characteristic of this mode of knowledge? Not only did Nostradamus see events and landscapes with their details, not only did he have an abstract perception of the harmonies and causalities of history, but it is as if something or someone were speaking within him, and addressing the part of our brains that is prepared and organized to receive articulated sounds and recognize their meaning. What do you think?"

"Unless we assume that 'Varennes' came to him from reading a map," said de Momordy, "or 'Herne' from a signpost, or 'Saulce' from an oil merchant's sign, we certainly have to acknowledge that some inner ear was involved."

"How can we interpret this observation except by acknowledging that the two senses that provide long-distance perceptions and simultaneously the alchemy of language were summoned up in the brain of Nostradamus by the 'revelation' transcribed in the quatrains that interest us? I emphasize 'in the brain.' We are not trifling with the cutaneous, extraretinal vision of a scholar like Farigoule!"

"Probably you are right," de Momordy went on. "But, if you assume that the 'revelation' was seen, heard, and even thought and developed through what you call the alchemy of language, you run into trouble, or at least a major question."

"Perhaps I've foreseen it. Which one?"

"Nostradamus wrote in decasyllabic, rhymed lines in which the final silent syllables are always elided except at the cesura, after the fourth syllable. All the quatrains of the *Centuries* are poured into this mold. What is the relationship between what he heard from his 'source' and what he wrote down? We find ourselves in a situation that is less simple than that of Victor Hugo, who recited more or less poetic answers that he drew from the table at a séance. There Hugo provided everything—the unfailing style and prosody that he had created and, at the same time, no less Hugo-like, the contents of the words that he attributed in good faith to the spirits. In the *Centuries*, at least in quatrains 9.20 and 34, we know the content did not come from Nostradamus, or from him alone, because it has been verified by history, but the rhythmic structure, uniform from the beginning to the end of the collection, is his. Might he not have cut some here and added some there to make his Pythia fit the Procrustean bed?"

"You are right," said Espopondie. "That is a problem and I have some ideas about it. But we are getting away from the limited subject we had set for today, which does not concern the source or sources of the quatrains, but only, objectively, the characteristics of what they say. Put some more thought into the rest."

Charles Leslucas probably thought he discerned a bit of weariness in Espopondie's eyes. Moreover, we all had the impression that we were not getting anywhere, just bogging down in analysis.

"Before we part, sir," he said, "I should like to submit to you an idea I had, one not without some connection to our problem. Just now you recalled that the date 1792, as well as the two years around it, all fatal in different ways for the monarchy, can be read in black and white in the dedicatory epistle addressed to Henri II, king of France. Now, there are also a very few dated events scattered throughout the *Centuries* themselves. Curiously, they mostly concern distant populations. In 1607 (quatrain 2.54) there would be a battle among the Arabs of North Africa, and also (8.71), in a place not indicated, a persecution of 'astronomers.' In 1609, at the beginning of the year (10.91, with a final line that is incomplete), the Roman clergy 'shall make a choice of gray and black "de la Compagn[i]e yssu"'—and this is not necessarily about some conclave or some Jesuit pope, which would be wrong. October 1737 would see 'the king of Persia' captured by 'those of Egypt' and 'conflict, death, plague bring great shame to the Cross.' I have no information about any of that. But quatrain 1.49, after an incomplete and obscure line, records an important and verified event:

Beaucoup avant telles menees
Ceux d'Orient par la vertu lunaire
L'an mil sept cens feront grands emmenees
Subiungant presque le coing Aquilonaire.

(Much before these doings
Those of the East by virtue of the moon

> In the year 1700 shall carry multitudes away
> Subjugating almost the northern corner.)

"Now here is something I have just remarked in *History of Russia* by Brian-Chaninov, which a friend of mine at the École Gaxotte showed me in manuscript, and which I expect will soon be published by Arthème Fayard. It concerns Peter the Great, who up to this point had been mostly busy with Turkey and the Streltsy.

> The year 1700 inaugurated the long sequence of wars against Sweden. In 1699, the secret treaty with August of Poland obliged Russia upon signing the Turkish treaty to invade Finland, Karelia, and Ingria. [But the Turkish peace could not be completed until August 1700.] Instead of attacking Finland, Peter took advantage of this time lapse to reorganize his army in a modern style. Toward the middle of 1700 he succeeded in creating two well-equipped, well-armed divisions. Forty thousand men were moved toward the frontier with Sweden, but rather than marching against Finland, they were sent beneath the walls of Narva, the taking of which could threaten Estonia and Livonia. The siege of the spot was set back, however, and the Russians did not open fire on the citadel until the end of September. This delay allowed Charles XII to defeat the Danes and land in Estonia. During the night of November 17–18 the Russians were stupefied to learn that the Swedes were approaching Narva on a forced march. Peter panicked.

"He turned the command over to a new leader, the prince of Croy, and the result of 'this sort of desertion' was not long in coming: 'The eight thousand exhausted and starving Swedes quickly overcame the forty thousand Russians. It was a disaster and, for Peter, a harsh lesson that he never forgot. Charles XII, however, delighted with having so easily gotten the better of his adversary, would not deign to pursue him, and the Russians escaped a complete rout.' Yes, disaster. Peter with his 'quite Oriental' Muscovites only 'almost' subjugated the northern corner—a nice definition of the northern sea we call the Baltic, of this acute angle pushed between the lands, from Denmark to Lapland. But starting in 1700, Peter raised two new armies, which he entrusted to two good generals and whose value increased from year to year. Several more armies would be required, along with the routing of Charles XII at Poltava, for the 'almost' of 1700 to be transformed into a secure fact. In a few months, Riga, Pernau, Dinamünde, and even the Finnish Viborg fell into the hands of the Russians (1708). Six years later, the destruction of the Swedish fleet in the naval battle of Hangöudd and the occupation of most of Finland would force Charles XII to make peace—temporary peace. It was only in 1721 that the heir to Charles XII would recognize, through the treaty of Nystadt, the czar's possession of Estonia, Livonia, Karelia, the Viborg district, and all the islands in the Gulf of Riga and those belonging to Finland. All that Sweden would retain in the upper portion of the 'northern corner' was Finland almost in its entirety and the islands in the Gulf of Bothnia."

Charles Leslucas seemed very content with his discovery. He emphasized that so far as he knew, no commentator had recognized that this quatrain dealt with this event of 1700, with its incalculable consequences: the entrance of Muscovite Russia into European debates.

We could only congratulate him and hope he would find equally neat explanations for the African events of 1607 and 1727, as well as for the electoral activity of the 'Roman clergy' in 1609.

But this excursus had led us away from the quatrain about Varennes, even though it posed in part the same problems, as much through its synthetic view of complicated events as through the way it disguised the Baltic Sea in a periphrasis that was really quite transparent. So we talked about something else, putting off to our next meeting the examination of what Espopondie had proposed for us: the essential.

6

Two days went by without Espopondie's mentioning the *Centuries* to me again. I, for my part, was thinking it over. The second evening during supper I broke the silence. We were supposed to see our friends again the next day and I hoped to have a little better knowledge of what the master of the house intended to lay before us.

"At the end of one of our last meetings you said it was time to start talking about the essential element. But it seems to me that we have more than begun already. What of this 'essential' still remains? What can we say tomorrow?"

"All that I shall do, myself," said Espopondie, "is merely repeat what I thought long ago after scribbling the paper that you read: I don't know, I don't understand. The 'essential' thing to do would be, yes, to work at discovering the *cur* [why] after the *quomodo* [how] and basically the *quomodo* after the *quale* [what]. But we have to stick with the *quale*, I think. Once more we shall have observed the phenomenon, the appearance, possibly the surface, but the mechanism, the reality, will have eluded us. I should, however, like to hear our friends hold forth on the subject of this 'essential.'"

"That is indeed what I expected," I said, "and I want to do the same thing. But I have scratched the surface a little more. Maybe I have located the point at least through which Nostradamus had access to the archives of the future, or was invaded by them—a sort of replica, in the direction of the future, of what the Romans called the *mundus* [world]."

"I'm listening."

"All in all, everything happens as if Nostradamus's brain, flying acrobatically from one to the other, functioned over several time periods. He plays with recorded and retained events the same way you shuffle cards, replacing chronological order with other orders, ones that are intellectual, emotional, or perhaps aesthetic. The best example basically is still 'the black monk.' In chronological order, the detention of Louis XVI at the Temple should be evoked *after* his 'coming within Varennes,' the way it is taught in textbooks. From the point of view of a literary critic, when he sets the allusion to captivity *before* Varennes, by designating the future guest at the Temple as the present agent of this 'coming within Varennes,' Nostradamus, or his source, accomplishes something very effective. It is as if he were saying: Unfortunate man, he doesn't know what awaits him; he doesn't realize that Varennes is a trap! How can he be warned that this will all end up in the Temple?"

"Let's not repeat ourselves. Where do you mean to go with this?"

"Despite this freedom in making use of what he knows, *all* the elements of this knowledge are just as they could have been perceived or imagined by Louis XVI himself at one time or another. Including what I just said: imprisoned in the Temple, the king could think 'Ah, if I had known, I would not have changed Fersen's plan, I would not have taken the wrong road, the one to Sainte-Menehould . . .' He could also have compared his sorry state to the luxury that even very recently surrounded the great prior of the black monks. Because he knew his French history, he, as we believe Nostradamus did, could feel and explore the analogy between his situation and Childéric's, and, as he went over the seventh-century murder in his mind, he could bitterly regret the 'division' that, a year and a half earlier, in this same place, at Bondy, had separated him from the skillful and daring Swede. Those could have been his 'thoughts.'

"As for the 'feelings,' he had, map in hand, noticed and identified everything during the journey, and consequently also the white chalk in Champagne that went on forever. He had seen Varennes and knew Narbonne and Sauce only too well—Sauce whom he had considered to be his savior at first, and had even thanked in a letter from Paris, but whose stupidity and duplicity, whose 'betrayal,' he was able to assess once he was captured, just as he had been more and more able to persuade himself that Narbonne had 'betrayed' him. Wearing on his head the Phrygian cap, he saw with his eyes the Louvre overrun, the attack of Barbaroux's five hundred men, which had made him take refuge with his enemies in the Assembly; he had felt fire and blood. And what was he thinking at the moment at which the 'blade' fell on his neck?"

"Come to your conclusion."

"I come to no conclusion, but I feel that I have chanced upon the entrance to a *mundus* that is inside out, through which the men of the future could communicate with the men of the present, Louis XVI of 1791 or 1793 with sixteenth-century Nostradamus. How and where did Nostradamus get this knowledge of what, two hundred fifty years later, would be the experiences and perhaps the reflections of the king? Well, here is one way, crazy but still a way. Suppose not only that Nostradamus had the benefit of more than normal lucidity as far as the fate of the dynasty he held in high regard was concerned, but also that he was in direct communication with the brain of the future Louis XVI as it registered and ruminated . . ."

"You worry me. That would be a strange method for transmitting thought. Through the successive seed of the descendants of Henri IV, cousin of his beloved Valois, the brain of Nostradamus would have been informed through the adult neurons of Louis XVI, who had yet to wait two hundred years to be born!"

"I said that only to indicate one possible means of access to the mystery. If there were some transmission of thought between two human beings, it could only be this particular one and between these two persons. We were admiring how Nostradamus articulated the times, setting them in mirrors or separating them into isolated groups, but this would have been less trouble (and more normal, if I may say so, because it would have concerned *his* own experiences and *his* own fate) if this time it took place in the future brain of Louis XVI, preexisting in some seed that transmitted it to the brain of Nostradamus, his contemporary."

"If you don't mind, let's eliminate this transmission of thought between the germinal ancestor of a future spermatozoid and the brain of a living adult. What other access to the mystery did you find? What other *mundus*?"

"Revelation, but that presupposes some theology. Neither of us is well disposed toward angels of annunciation."

"What do you have left?"

"Recourse to the strictest determinism. Your and my impression of free will, in every case, without exception, would be completely illusory, only justified by the frightful complexity of the processes. Everything could, in principle, be expressed in algebraic form, but it would require billions and billions of equations. However, just as there exist at our level people who are astoundingly good at calculating figures, we might think that prophets, ours at least, from time to time have an infinitely greater ability to master and instantly combine the elements of this immense mass and thus to 'tell' the future."

"At least your third *mundus* has in its favor that it is cloaked in the language of mechanics. But are you considering the power that you attribute to your oracle givers? Despite his billions of neurons, what Nostradamus had in his brain, the information imparted by his education and his own life, was limited! Specifically, we know of no connection between him and the Bourbons, the cousins of the Valois. Then don't you have to assume that his algebraic machinery could, according to a determinism linking everything to everything else, step by step, have access to an unlimited number of facts external to his brain, to sorts of information banks built up in other brains that are, in principle, made like his but lacking his gift of instantaneous, total calculation that masters number, time, and space? This would be another form of thought transmission, less bizarre than the other because it would be exerted among contemporary, adult 'thinkers.' In short, your three *mundi* come down to two: revelation, which you rule out, and exteriorized thought, and you imagine two varieties of the latter."

"My good professor," I said, "you have taught me that the only science is the science of phenomena. So let's say that what I'm doing is literature. But you also taught me that in essence science is a conqueror, that we live surrounded by kinds of actions and agents about which we have no more idea today than Aristotle had about electric current or the Curies' radiation. Barring some unforeseeable invention we shall, perhaps, never know what goes on at every point in time, in every component of our nervous system and in the links that exist between these points. But we shall make enough progress to catch a glimpse of how our prophet, soaked in—flooded by—'data,' worked."

"Well, look how wise you have turned out! But I quite enjoyed your little attack of imagination. You see, I too sometimes let myself go in dreaming, and I do above all try to keep from erasing or denying things I can't explain. To tell you the absolute truth, I am willing to believe in the transmission of thought, without explaining it. Listen, two or three years ago my old friend and mentor Doctor Richet, a great force behind studies in parapsychology and an impeccably honest man, told me this. He had just gone to Warsaw to examine a famous medium, whose name was Guzik, I believe. In Warsaw, at the home of the ambassador, M. de Panafieu, everyone was in agreement, warning him to be careful: several times the medium had been caught red-handed in fraud. Nothing could be more natural, he replied. Every time 'they' can come out on top without too much trouble by faking or using special effects, they do so, because it saves them effort and fatigue; it is all a matter of verification. Indeed, in broad daylight and before the suspicious eyes of several witnesses, he kept a perfect check on the medium. Before he left Paris he had asked the great Sarah Bernhardt to write a few words on a piece of paper that she then placed in an envelope. She herself had sealed the envelope without saying what was in it. Richet handed the message to the medium, who held and fingered it for a long time, a very long time, several hours if I remember correctly, with no possibility of opening it or looking at it against the light. Finally, he gave up: 'I can't tell you what is written. I only know that it is about darkness and light.' Richet opened the envelope. Sarah had written a line from *Chantecler*: 'It is at night that it is lovely to believe in light.'

"Richet is neither a liar nor a fool. He intends to publish this 'scientific observation' in a book, but no one will pay any attention. I think we have to deposit it in the 'data bank' without comment."

Espopondie had never spoken to me in such clear terms about what he called "secondary physics," which, if generations of observers would be patient, was gradually replacing metaphysics. I expressed my surprise. "So you allow that there can be science even when what is being studied cannot be reproduced at will?"

"The science of today, no. But the science of the future, perhaps. A correctly observed fact is a fact to be recorded and held in reserve, even if it is—permanently or for the time being—quantitatively unique and qualitatively singular, whether by nature or because it eludes capture by our instruments. The case of quatrains 20 and 34 of century 9, for that matter, is of another sort. From now on it really is 'scientific material,' although science does not know how to approach it. Although we are unable to reproduce at will the 'work' of Nostradamus, we can at least reread and dissect his text as often and with as many perspectives as we wish, indefinitely confronting the ever more familiar detail about what it seems to predict, drawing up and rectifying at our leisure tables of agreements and contradictions. What makes these quatrains material worth singling out is that the list of agreements is well stocked and the list of contradictions empty. All that is missing is the hookup with our knowledge as a whole, and first with what we know about the human nervous system."

"Do you think there is anything worth retaining of the things that Nostradamus, in his prose writings, claimed to be revealing about his work, his sources, astrological calculations, and so forth?"

"Even if he is sincere, he confuses the issue. Anyway, what a lot of nonsense! Read the preface of 1558."

I flipped through the pages of Le Pelletier and came upon these sentences:

> The secrets of God are incomprehensible, and their effective power belongs to a sphere far remote from natural knowledge; for, deriving their immediate origin from the free will, things make evident causes that of themselves could never attract the attention that could make them recognized, either by human augury, or by any other knowledge of occult power.

And somewhat further along:

> The perfect knowledge of causes cannot be acquired without divine inspiration, because all prophetic inspiration derives its first motive principle from God the Creator, next from good fortune, and then from nature.

The next day, as he greeted Momordy and Leslucas, Espopondie summarized our meanderings for them and had me read two or three pages from Nostradamus's preface.

"Your turn to speechify, my friends. As for me, I'm still right where I was at the beginning, capable at most of zeroing in, as you say, marking the opening to the *mundus* with guardrails and a sign reading 'danger.'"

Our friends did not seem terribly keen. Leslucas simply said that although he was impressed by the list of accordant evidence, he was just as—or even more—convinced than we were that any attempt at explanation *hic et nunc* [here and now] was futile. Metaphysics was irrelevant to his life, and he was unconcerned with "secondary physics"; he lived very well in this manner, as something of a stoic and something of an epicurean. Through training and by profession, he limited himself to establishing facts.

De Momordy seemed quite uncomfortable. "You are both library men," he said sharply. "And your problems, even the jolts of life, are absorbed by your philological cushions. As for us, we are mowed down by the machinery of action. In a few months I shall take up my post, confronting Mustafa Kemal or some other monster of history. I shall have to make decisions, give advice . . ."

He took time to catch his breath, perhaps hesitating. "A god is a necessity for me, and your two quatrains do not distract me from this need. None of the things you put forward to contradict Nostradamus's humble avowals can do away with them: 'all prophetic inspiration derives its first motive principle from God the Creator.' After God come the principal archangels: 'good fortune,' let's say probability theory, and 'nature,' the life force *[l'élan vital]*, as they teach at the Collège de France."

There was a silence that we were careful not to disturb. Then he flared up again: "Why do you dismiss with a word what you refer to as theologies? You avoid even naming finality, yet to me both the need for this and its obviousness feel as strong as they are indefinable. Your determinism and your causality appending everything both ignore that: final causes . . . Besides, why do you question something as simple and useful as the distinction between body and spirit? You say our experience encounters no thought or will or love outside neurons, independent of neurons. What do you know about it? That's the whole problem.

"And you yourselves, ruling over your billions of neurons, what do you do about the impression of unity that is no more to be scorned than the rest of your experience? Listen, to be honest, I have the impression of living in a perpetual, universal fairyland, where things that can be explained are the exception. It seems to me that the normal is to the marvelous as the circle is to the ellipse: a specific instance, skimpy and impoverished, gutted of everything that makes conics powerful. Your ordinary trigonometry looks great next to these two focal points, this sine and cosine—both elliptical—whose relationship can only be expressed in a formula if you dare write in a little 'i,' the sign of an imaginary number whose content you cannot imagine. Is the square root of −1 any more rational or thinkable than the action of a god on your soul? Both are proven by their effectiveness.

"What's more, you make me laugh. Because the minute you start philosophizing you don't want to talk about memory and matter, mind and body, whereas you are perfectly happy to use these old words on an everyday basis. They are unsuitable, inadequate, archaic? They don't get to the 'bottom of things'? Fine. But they provide a perspective on the world that has the advantage of existing. We have to live! The French language is not exact, nor is any other, and yet we accomplish something when we talk; the vocabulary of one language never covers the vocabulary of another exactly, and yet we translate . . . In short, to get back to our prophet, I think he quite simply saw, heard, and thought through the grace of some god."

"The grace of God?"

"If you will. I don't deny this companion of my childhood. Besides," de Momordy added, blushing, "I too know something about the world of prophecy, from experience."

He no doubt expected us to ask him about it. But we did not, and Espopondie ended things by saying: "You have brought our debate to a close courageously. I like courage as much as prudence."

All three of us continued to meet in the company of our friend twice a week, but neither Varennes nor Sauce slipped into our conversation again. To cut short any further talk on the subject, moreover, Espopondie had, on that very evening of the last discussion, presented me with a gift—poisoned or precious, I cannot say: the paper that had been so much on our minds.

7 I

Toward the end of the winter of 1924–25, Espopondie's health deteriorated. Two diseases, his two Fates, requiring mutually exclusive conjurations, fought over which would have the honor of finishing him off. To distract him, de Momordy, Charles Leslucas, and I, who all owed him a great deal, continued to meet once or twice a week around his armchair, and we talked about "something else." I do not know what the incident was in February that steered us back to Nostradamus, but this time, as a sort of game, we decided that each of us in turn would imagine, would create on the basis of the *Centuries*, some event in the near future. Espopondie would award the prize to the one submitting the construction that was the simplest, the most literal, the most coherent, and at the same time the least plausible. Because I was just barely the eldest, they asked me to go first.

I have no talent for parlor games, and little imagination. I made a few vain attempts and then botched my assignment. Because I was then interested in the prose and verse produced by ancient Scandinavians to describe the end of the world, I chose the well-known quatrain 72 of century 10, one of the rare ones containing a date:

L'an mil neuf cens nonante neuf sept mois
Du ciel viendra un grand Roy d'effrayeur

(In the year nineteen-hundred and ninety-nine and seven months
From the sky shall come a great and terrifying King)

And I made it into some paradoxically optimistic apocalypse that I cannot even remember. Aren't the last words of the quatrain "by good fortune"? Espopondie smiled politely, but de Momordy pointed out that I had certainly made it easy for myself by inventing some mythology, whereas they were expecting history. Feeling eliminated, I did not defend myself. So we spent the rest of the afternoon talking about Paul Valéry's first *Cahier*, just published in facsimile by Champion.

The next week, Charles Leslucas, my young friend from the École Normale, had his turn. He was obsessed with deciphering the writings of Mycenaean Crete, but was having no success. Naturally he had chosen quatrain 89 of century 3, in which Crete's twin island, Cyprus, is mentioned.

En ce temps la sera frustree Cypres
De son secours de ceux de mer Egee:
Vieux trucidez, mais par mesles et lyphres
Seduict leur Roy, Royne plus outragee.

(At the time Cyprus shall be frustrated
Of its help from those of the Aegean Sea,
Old ones shall be killed, but by Mesles and Lipre,
Their king shall be seduced, and the queen more wronged.)

"I hope, at least, to satisfy you regarding implausibility," he said. "Cyprus is now in the hands of the English, who are preparing to transform their protectorate into a colonial regime, but I am going to assume that it has become independent and a completely separate nation. Greece has just established itself as a republic, but I am going to impose a dynasty upon it once again. Now, here is my event.

"Cyprus has a population composed, as you know, of Greeks and Turks, who up to now have been getting along more or less. But after the independence that I am conferring upon them, the Turks on the Continent, stirring up the Cypriot Turks, will begin to make demands and soon will occupy the portion directly opposite their shores, and even a little more. The royal government that I have reestablished in Athens, despite being the master of all the Aegean archipelagos, either will not dare provide or will be incapable of providing the Cypriot Greeks with the expected aid. There will be much violence—even murders—throughout the island. As far as the kingdom is concerned, during (and because of) the sad developments following the forced overcrowding of a population and an invading army, the king of Greece—'their' king, who can only be the king of 'those of the Aegean sea'—will be badly advised, and a queen—the wife or mother of the aforesaid king, you choose—will become more and more unpopular. I would not be surprised to see this lead, step by step, to a new expulsion of the king. But I am not inserting this ending into Nostradamus!"

Espopondie smiled again. De Momordy and I both said we were impressed. We agreed that this scenario had the required qualities of coherence and implausibility, but we objected that it could not be called literal, because the text contained obscure words, nor was the reading simple, because it had taken some pains to string together so many incidents in so few words. De Momordy attacked the exactness of the translation to begin with.

"Isn't the syntax of your interpretation arbitrary?" he asked. "You invent four sentences where there is only one verb."

"Nostradamus liked that sort of ellipsis," said Leslucas. "The verb of the first sentence, of the first line, *shall be*, multiplies throughout the rest: the old men *shall be* killed, the king *shall be* seduced, the queen *shall be* wronged."

"That's not all," de Momordy replied. "Your quatrain contains artificial terms invented by Nostradamus, and this gives you too much freedom—such as when you interpret 'mesles et lyphres' as 'the sad events resulting from the overcrowding of the occupiers and the occupied.'"

"My friend," Leslucas replied, "this is the translation that is called for. *Lyphre*, as indeed Le Pelletier saw eighty years ago, is obviously a forgery by some Hellenist. Its origins are made clear by the *y*, and the pointless *h* in *ph*—serving no purpose, because the rhyme is *ipre*—

just rubs this in, if you will pardon the slang. *Les lyp[h]res* can only be the Greek *ta lypra*—that is, things that make you sad or depressed. And look at the appropriateness of the word, even though it is suggested by the rhyme (*Cypres* is demanding!). It establishes a presentiment of the fatal, natural link between the sound of the name for Cyprus and the ordeal that will afflict it. We are reminded of this other line, preserved in a biography of Sophocles, I think, in which Ulysses, pursued by Fate, cries out (I have changed it a bit): 'Yes, for good reason I am called Odysseus, a name whose root is the same as that of suffering—*odynē*.' Nor are we surprised to find here a Greek word with French spelling; the event is Greek.

"As for *mesles*, this is one of those short substantives that Nostradamus tends to get from infinitives, preferring them to derivatives or longer compound words: *la pille* is his word for *le pillage*, or booty; *le part*, as we saw earlier, is *le départ* [departure]. *Mesle*, the equivalent of *mélange* [mixture], is none other than the second element of our *pêle-mêle*, which can also be found in the *Centuries* (10.98d: *pesle-mesle*). Combining this word with *lyp[h]res* is satisfying. At this moment, what causes the affliction of the Greeks of Cyprus, and as an indirect consequence the Greeks of Greece, unless it is, in fact, this interpenetration, this forced cohabitation with the Muslim invaders, this civil and military melee? This time the 'quatrain of Nantes' comes to mind (5.33: 'Cris, hurlements à Nantes piteux voir!' [Cries and howlings at Nantes it shall be piteous to see!]). It appears to describe the proconsul Carrier's famous 'mariages nantais' in the third line: 'Détranchés masles, infelice meslée' [Males cut in quarters, unhappy melee]. If you wish, you can translate this directly as 'through the overcrowdings *and* appalling events,' which does not change the sense at all. But this seems to me more like a hendiadys, juxtaposing cause and effect rather than placing them in a dependent construction: 'the appalling results *of the* overcrowdings.'

"We are left with the preposition *par*, which introduces 'mesles et lyp[h]res.' I understand it in the sense of 'through the fault of, on the occasion of,' and also, in a temporal sense, 'throughout the time of' (as we might say 'during our times' or 'nowadays'); but you can also translate it as an instrumental, as long as you bring the verb *séduire* [seduce] back to its original meaning: 'The king will be seduced, led away from sound politics, through the sad events of Cyprus.' I prefer my interpretation, however. I think I can read between the lines that if the king strays it is because he is 'seduced' by the advice of the queen, whether wife or mother, who is mentioned right after him and whom the people have good cause to treat worse and worse. This of course is not the same as the 'seduction' discussed in another quatrain, which was no less fatal to the king:

> Luxe, ô salle d'ébène où, pour séduire un roi,
> Se tordent dans leur mort des guirlandes funèbres,
> Vous n'êtes qu'un orgueil menti par les ténèbres
> Aux yeux du solitaire ébloui de sa foi.
>
> (Wealth, oh ebony hall where funeral garlands
> twist together to seduce a king in their death,
> You are merely pride, the lie of shadows
> In the eyes of a recluse dazzled by his faith.)

"And yet you must admit that our two lines, 'Old ones shall be killed, but by Mesles and Lipre, / Their king shall be seduced, and the queen more wronged,' seem particularly fine."

"Nostradamus really makes you think of Mallarmé?"

"And Baudelaire too. Listen:

> Le corps sans âme plus n'être en sacrifice,
> Jour de la mort mis en nativité:
> L'esprit divin fera l'âme félice
> Voyant le Verbe en son éternité.
>
> (The body without soul shall be no more in sacrifice,
> Day of death placed on the birthday,
> The divine spirit shall make the soul happy,
> Seeing the Word in its eternity.)"

The third week, de Momordy performed according to the rules:

"You are going to see," he said, "I have not slipped into any of your mistakes. My quatrain is lucid, my interpretation literal, and my material historical."

Jacques de Momordy was a young diplomat who was about to receive his first important post, and he expected it to be Ankara. He had prepared for this by completing his studies on the Near East, and he read and spoke Turkish reasonably well. Devilishly romantic, he would have preferred to see the Turkey of seraglios and caïques, but he was delighted by the idea of spending two or three summer months on the shores of the Bosporus, even if they were republican. It was no surprise, therefore, to hear him speak of Istanbul in relation to quatrain 97 of century 2:

Romain pontife garde de t'approcher
De la cité que deux fleuves arrouse,
Ton sang viendra auprès de la cracher,
Toy et les tiens, quand fleurira la rose.

(Roman pontiff beware of approaching
The city watered with two rivers,
Thou shalt spit there thy blood
Thou and thine when the rose shall bloom.

De Momordy went straight to the point: "Here is my translation," he said. "Holy Father, beware of approaching the city that pours the water of its streams and its runoff into the Bosporus and into the Golden Horn. (If you do so despite this warning) shortly thereafter, some day in May, the consequence will be that your blood will gush onto yourself and onto your entourage."

Then his commentary:

"The visit of a head of the Roman Catholic Church to the opposite pole of Christianity, conquered by Islam, or even the fact of his merely entering Turkey, would, I imagine, be taken as a provocation by some Muslim fanatic who, from that moment on, would have only one idea—to kill him. A few months or a few years later, somewhere, some day in May, either alone or manipulated, this individual would try his luck, if I may be so bold as to put it that way, and severely wound the Holy Father, along with several bystanders."

We all felt that de Momordy had won the prize. But Charles Leslucas needed to get revenge. He came up with repeated quibbles:

"I see in the second line, in Le Pelletier, not *qui*, a subject, but *que*, an object."

"That doesn't change anything. Nostradamus sometimes uses *que* in the nominative, for *qui*—a survival from the Middle Ages. At any rate, the relative pronoun is the subject because the verb *arrouse* is in the singular."

"And can the Bosporus and the Golden Horn really be said to be rivers?"

"They are in the strictest sense of the word, even though they are rivers with 'odd peculiarities,' as Verlaine describes some of his loves. The Bosporus is nothing but a large canal created by the confluence of all the rivers feeding the Black Sea, from the Danube to the Phasis. The Black Sea itself is only an engorgement, a reservoir, contained by the long dam created by the coasts of Thrace and Anatolia. In ancient times the dam opened in one place and the water found a way out. Yes, the Bosporus is a river with the largest rivers of Europe as its tributaries. You would know it if you had felt how strong the flow is near Bébek, resulting in what the local inhabitants call 'the Devil's Current.' As for the Golden Horn, widened and worn away as a fjord, it is only the common estuary of two quite modest rivers today, making up what are still called 'the Freshwaters of Europe.'"

"But why privilege Istanbul? More than one city in the world discharges its water, both clean and dirty, into two rivers. Hasn't Lyon, for example, at the confluence of the Saône and the Rhône, been suggested?"

"You can read the 'city with two rivers' any way you wish, but you will have to discover the reason that a 'Roman pontiff' would run risks there that are specific to his function, connected to his title, which is solemnly pronounced in the first words of the first quatrain, with the adjective *Roman* obviously underscored. You could, for example, choose seven-gated Thebes from Greek epics, that being the one that the chorus in *The Suppliants* calls 'polis dipotamos' because of its two rivers, the Asope and the Ismène. A humanist pope might well be tempted to make a pilgrimage to the home of Pindar. Why not? But how could this whim provoke a murderous reaction?

Whereas the great mosque of Saint-Sophia filled with the coats of arms of the prophet's successors, the patriarch of the Second Rome confined within the Phanar in Constantinople, Islam defending what remains of its former conquests against any stray impulse toward, or any appearance of, a crusade—altogether, these form the small core of a war of religion justifying to a certain extent the incident that I imagine."

"Are you sure that the two halves of the quatrain are so closely linked? Perhaps the bloody incident described in the second is just by chance *subsequent to* but not *logically caused by* the visit advised against in the first."

"The general applicability of the expression 'Roman pontiff beware' suggests that the danger is permanent, not personal, hence simultaneously linked to the function of the prospective traveler and to the nature of the city he must not go near. The *Centuries* contain two other quatrains that are also warnings introduced by the imperative of the verb *garder* [reflexively, beware]. One of them (3.43) is constructed like the one we are considering. It comes down to: 'People of the southwest of France, beware of crossing the Apennine Mountains; (otherwise) you will die and be buried in Rome and in Ancona.' The threat is not veiled. Nostradamus imagines a military expedition (the fourth line speaks of a trophy raised) doomed to disaster. The relationship of the two parts of the quatrain is obviously one of cause and effect. It is the same here."

"Fine," said Leslucas. "But something else is bothering me. You take 'auprès de là' in the third line as an indication of time meaning 'shortly thereafter.' But why would it not be, quite simply, an indication of place? The pontiff would be struck 'near' where his action took place, near the provocation."

"The warning is not merely impersonal, it is atemporal, with no limitation to one season or another, whereas the bleeding is predicted to take place in the spring, 'when the rose will bloom.' That makes no sense unless the effect, thus restricted to a season, is not of necessity immediately temporally juxtaposed to its cause, whose date is undetermined and immaterial, and whose effect, consequently, can be produced in another place. If the expression 'auprès de là' bothers you because it seems strictly and doubly local—doubly through the *auprès* [near] and the *là* [there], I send you back to Nostradamus for reassurance, because he has used it elsewhere in a context in which it is unquestionably temporal. In 3.33a–b, we read '*En* la cité où le loup entrera / *Bien près de là* les ennemis seront' [In the city where the wolf will enter / Very near there the enemies will be]. Because one cannot simultaneously be 'in' and 'near' a place, these lines mean 'when the wolf shall come into the city in question, the enemies will be there too, very shortly thereafter.'"

"There is, however, in the third line of our quatrain about the pontiff, '*viendra* auprès de là' [shall come near there]. Doesn't the *shall come*, a verb of movement, oblige us to keep a sense of place for 'auprès de là'?"

"You are mutilating the line. It doesn't say 'viendra auprès de là.' *Venir* is only there to support the infinitive that follows, *viendra cracher*, in a construction that is frequently found in the *Centuries* and that usually means 'to come with the intention of,' which is impossible here because the pontiff's blood will not 'come' anywhere 'in order to' burst forth, or, in a more general sense, it will not 'come' anywhere at all. Hence what we have here is a future periphrastic, which is more solemn than 'your blood will burst forth.' 'Your blood will come to burst forth' suggests something like 'your blood, conforming to and obeying the destiny that I utter, shall burst forth.' Or, less mythologically, 'it shall happen that your blood bursts forth.' The words 'auprès de là' provide an additional nuance: 'il ad-viendra dans un a-venir proche' [it will come to pass in a nearby time to come]."

"All right. But it seems to me that you have been very free in your construing of 'toy et les tiens' [thou and thine] by assuming that it is only the pope's blood that will splash not merely *on* him but *on* his entourage: where is the word *on*? Isn't this rather a reworking of the subject of the sentence: 'Your blood will burst—yes, your blood and that of your people'?"

"I'm not the one freely construing these four words; they have been freely construed by Nostradamus. This is not the first time he has used this nonspecific, sometimes breathless syntax to begin laying out information about the circumstances. He puts them in parentheses, without saying what justifies them or what relationship they have with some more important element or another in the sentence. You may perhaps be right, then, that the pontiff will not be the only one who bleeds. Upon reflection, that is even an interesting variant: either the pope, the only one wounded, will bleed on himself and those who attend him, or else other individuals, members of the pontiff's staff or faithful strangers who have come to see him, will bleed as he does, with him. The two scenes moreover can be combined. Let's compromise, if you like: at the same time that the pope bloodies his entourage, a pious tourist, let's say an American woman for good measure, will collapse, struck by another bullet or another stroke of the knife."

"I accept," said Leslucas. "But are you sure that 'when the rose shall bloom' is to be taken in the literal sense, as an indication of the season? The rose has served as the symbol for so many ideas! Might it not mean here a political spring, the electoral victory, for example, of a sort of advanced democracy, not so red as that of a scholar like Herriot, but a slightly deeper color than what Poincaré proposed?"

"De minimis non curat vates [the soothsayer pays no attention to the little people]," said de Momordy. "Besides, there is the golden rule: stick to the most natural sense within the context. The quatrains contain enough obscurities for us to treat the few lanterns hung in their darkness with respect."

Espopondie had let us go on, but the debate was flagging. He brought it to a close.

"You are the winner," he told the diplomat. "Your scene is the most sober and your interconnections are the best, and the event you have thought up is by far the most improbable. How would a pope have either the notion or the possibility of going to Istanbul—of going anywhere at all outside Rome? Because, since 1870, no matter who reigned, the 'Roman pontiffs' have regarded themselves as prisoners within the confines of the Vatican, and Benito Mussolini is no man to deprive the kingdom of its capital city. As far as the Turks are concerned, any such movement of religious fanaticism is almost unimaginable now that Mustafa Kemal, who has already sent the sultan away and abolished the rule of the caliphs, is working so energetically to Europeanize and secularize his country. He has replaced Friday as the day of rest with Sunday; he sends imams who dare preach against the wearing of hats to the gallows; he has closed the convents of the dervishes; he will not even let a mosque be built in Ankara, and I have heard that Arab writing will not be around much longer. Yes, my friend, your idea is the nuttiest. You win."

We were about to change the subject when I heard him mutter: "Still . . . who knows?"

8

This fresh eruption of our Nostradamian games did not persist, although we four continued to meet. But one day as I was digging through the already considerably thinner sediment of papers that had thrived in one of the rooms of the apartment, I came upon a few pages with the title "A Source of Nostradamus: Titus-Livy."

"Ah, I had completely forgotten that!" said Espopondie. "This business about sources is not related to any form of 'secondary physics,' and it was not written to give credit to Nostradamus. It proves that, given the chance, Michel de Damenôtre did the same thing as the Polish medium Charles Richet did—he cheated. Or precisely, he made things up, or at least cheerfully enriched the future with the past. Roman institutions, and the history of Rome as it had been produced by antiquarians and annalists, were at least as familiar to him as they are to well-read individuals today—or more so. The humanists of the Renaissance were all brought up on Aulu-Gelle, the remnants of Varro, the summary of Verrius Flaccus, without mentioning Titus-Livy or Plutarch. Every citizen of the republic of letters, whether moralist or poet, philosopher or medical doctor, benefited from this knowledge according to the art he practiced. Why not fortunetellers? Consequently, I was not terribly surprised fifteen or twenty years ago to find out that the first mention made by French literature of this triad of the greatest flamens (the flamens have always intrigued me, and I recommend the subject to you) is in Nostradamus. At the same time I recognized that the history of Rome, in Titus-Livy, was one of the sources of the future that this verbose prophet claimed to predict. Read me those pages again. They can't be very long."

I read them:

It is generally acknowledged that century 5 of the oracles was published immediately following the death of Nostradamus. Now in it there is a rare occurrence: a series of quatrains (numbered from 74 to 82) that do not require too much skill to be connected to one single event, predicted in vague terms—that is, the arrival of a prestigious individual who will be simultaneously a restorer and a reformer of the Church, and a "great legislator" in general (79):

74: De sang troyen naistra coeur Germanique
Qui deviendra en si haute puissance
Hors chassera [gent] estrange Arabique
Tournant l'Eglise en prestine preeminence
(obviously this should read 'eminence').

(Of Trojan blood shall be born a German heart
Who shall come into such a high power
He shall drive out the Arabic foreigners
Turning the Church into pristine preeminence.)

Although several of the quatrains following this entry (76, 78, 79, 80) do not provide any opening, two of them (75, 77) are completely clear. Here is the latter, which describes first a real metamorphosis, a paganization of the hierarchy of the Church, and then the intervention of a king of France:

Tous les degrez d'honneur Ecclesiastique
Seront changez en dial quirinal:
En Martial quirinal flaminique,
Puis vn Roy de France le rendra vulcanal.

(All the degrees of ecclesiastical honor
Shall be changed into a Quirinal Dial:
Into Martial Quirinal flaminus
Then a king of France shall make it vulcanal.)

In the second and third lines Nostradamus is referring to the Roman triad of the principal flamens—flamen Dial, flamen Martial, and flamen Quirinal—that is, the priests serving Jupiter, Mars, and Quirinus, with a strong stress on the hierarchical order in which they are presented. That, in fact, was the Roman doctrine of ordo sacerdotum, *the order of the priests, which was based on 'unequal honors,'* discrimina dignitatis. *We only need to recall the note provided by the abbreviator of Verrius Flaccus:*

> *[Among the priests] it is the* rex *who is considered the most important; then comes the* flamen Dialis, *after him the* Martialis, *in fourth place the* Quirinalis, *and in fifth the* pontifex maximus. *Consequently, during a meal, the* rex *is seated above all the priests, the* Dialis *above the* Martialis, *and the* Quirinalis *above the* pontifex. *The* rex *because he is the most powerful; the* Dialis *because he is priest of the universe that is known as* dium; *the* Martialis *because Mars is father of the founder of Rome; the* Quirinalis *because Quirinus was called from Cures to become part of the Roman Empire; the* pontifex maximus *because he is judge and arbiter of things both human and divine.*

The word flaminique *(pertaining to the flamen), which Nostradamus has put at the end of the list, is ambiguous. It can be a feminine substantive and designate, as was frequently the case in Rome,* the *feminine attribute par excellence of the flamen, the wife of the flamen Dialis. It can also be masculine and an adjective; in this case, it would constitute a common label, applicable to each of the three priests named in these two lines, who are without exception of the flamen type—that is, connected, each in his different way, to the precise zone of the sacred of which his eponymous god is patron. Given that the text introduces no feminine individual, the second explanation seems the more likely.*

The hierarchical factor is oddly marked. The low degree, "quirinal," is indeed mentioned twice in symmetrical expressions, in the second and third lines, but each time it is set in apposition to one of the degrees superior to it; these are both introduced in the traditional order, first Dial and then Martial.

It is not possible to be clear about how Nostradamus represented this paganization of the Christian ordo sacerdotum *to himself. It is paradoxical. Read literally, it is even inconceivable, because the definition of the flamens, particularly the three principal ones, presupposes a rigorous polytheism, with the supernatural divided into separate domains, each of which is the exclusive property and the field of action reserved for one of the great gods. In the theology of the Roman Republic, Jupiter, Mars, and Quirinus are best defined through their positive or negative relationships, their affinities and their oppositions. How, while remaining Christian, could the Church submit to having its sacred personnel split up and compartmentalized in this manner? It would not be simply an affair of organization and priorities; it would involve the unitary principle of its theology. Perhaps this question, which to us seems serious, would have had no meaning for Nostradamus, who was a philologist and not a theologian—and who, moreover, even in his philology certainly did not have a clear idea of the fundamental meaning of the triad of principal flamens. His text does not rise above wordplay, the picturesque association of Latin names in their traditional sequence.*

In principle, there are numerous possible sources for this passage, as numerous as the Latin texts that speak of the principal flamens, all of which were known in the middle of the sixteenth century. Although the expression 'all the degrees of ecclesiastical honor' makes one think of the beginning of the note by Festus that I copied (Lindsay's edition, 199), the context of quatrain 77 sends us back, rather, to the historians because it is about a "change," a reform meriting the creation of a new clergy—which is confirmed, two quatrains later (79), by the introduction of the author of this reform as a "legislator" ("through the coming of the great legislator"). This solemn word directs us toward a specific source: Nostradamus predicts that the return of the Church "in pristine eminence" will be the work of an exceptional man. From that point on, how can we avoid thinking of the founding of the institution of the three principal flamens by the king who, according to the epic legend of Rome, organized the priesthood—Numa Pompilius? This is what Titus-Livy says of him (1.20.1–2):

> *Next [= after the creation of the calendar of feast days], the establishment of the priesthood received his attention, although he himself performed most of the sacred acts, especially those assumed nowadays by the* flamen Dialis. *But, thinking that in a warlike city, kings resembled Romulus more often than Numa and went to war in person, he wanted to avoid having the cults dependent on the royal function ever being left with no one to serve them. This is why he created a flamen confined to his residence for Jupiter and honored him with a special costume and the curule chair belonging to the king. He added two other flamens to this one, one for Mars, the other for Quirinus.*

The hypothesis that Livy was the source is sustained in the odd seventy-fifth quatrain, which precisely describes the first deed of this individual, essentially a religious act:

> *Montera haut sur le bien [pour: lieu?] plus à dextre*
> *Demourera assis sur la pierre quarrée,*
> *Vers le midy posé à sa senestre*
> *Baston tortu en main, bouche serrée.*

> (He shall climb high on the good [place?], more to the right,
> He shall remain seated on the square stone,
> Toward the south, set on his left
> A bent stick in hand, mouth shut tight.)

We have only to refer to the first actions of Numa, described by Titus-Livy, to have the key to these four lines:

> *Led by an oracle . . . to the Capitol, he took his seat on a stone, turned toward the south. The oracle sat to his left, head veiled, holding in his right hand a bent, knotless stick called a lituus. [In his mind he divided the space into four parts, with the one in the south considered the right and the one in the north the left, and he fixed a landmark for himself.] Finally, passing the lituus into his left hand and placing his right on Numa's head, he spoke this prayer: "Jupiter if it is* fas *[divine law] that this man, Numa Pompilius, upon whose head I lay my hands, be king of Rome, I pray thee to send us clear and certain signs*

> *within the area that I have defined." Then he declared what auspices he wished to see sent. When they had been, Numa, declared king, descended from the sacred ground.*

When we put the two together, all of Nostradamus's expressions become clear. "Bent stick," a peculiar expression if it pertained—as has been suggested—to an Episcopal crosier, is the very definition of lituus, *and the "shut mouth" is not, as has also been suggested, a "physiological sign of inflexibility of character," but the* silentium *[silence] required for any taking of auspices. The "square stone" is the seat on which the* inauguratus *[consecrated one] sat while taking into account the four points of the compass. The first words, "he shall climb high," recall the fact that Numa's inauguration took place at one of the highest points of Rome, on the spot that was to become the* auguraculum *of the Capitol.*

I note only two differences, both important and certainly intentional: first, the two individuals, the seated king and the priest bearing the lituus, seem merged into one; second, the orientation of the person being inaugurated is not the same as that of Numa. These changes, especially the second, are no doubt meant to "depaganize" the scene. If the Christian restorer of Rome imagined by Nostradamus must, indeed, be inaugurated in the pagan manner, it is appropriate that it be done with at least some change in the code.

It certainly does seem, therefore, that Nostradamus was fully conscious of having modeled the bearing of his character upon Numa's and that of the augur, all according to Titus-Livy, the only author who has preserved for us the scenario of the inauguratio *[inauguration]. However, one slight puzzle still remains, located in the fourth line of quatrain 77. It is interesting as a puzzle, because, after the names of the three major flamens, it concerns a word that itself is particularly employed in Latin to designate a flamen, but a minor one, probably the first of the twelve minor flamens: Vulcan,* volcanalis. *What is the meaning of this final word, which apparently unsettles the enclosed structure of the three earlier lines?*

First, as we frequently find in Nostradamus, there is a syntactical difficulty that does not allow resolution. In the first three lines of quatrain 77 everything is in the plural, whether grammatically ("all the degrees," "they will be") or at least enumeratively ("dial quirinal," "Martial quiri-

nal flaminique"). So what can the singular le *[him or it] refer to when it pops up in the fourth line: "Then a king of France shall make him/it vulcanal"?*

On the other hand, what can it mean to make, or to become, "vulcanal"? What action is being attributed to a king of France? Vulcan, or Volcan, as employed by Nostradamus, is never other than what he was in Rome—that is, the patron of fire as a destructive force, or, by metonymy, the fire itself. Specifically, he is not a blacksmith, and "making someone vulcanal" could not mean, as some hasty commentators have supposed, "making someone invulnerable by creating impenetrable armor for him." Therefore, it would seem that the king of France relegates to the fire, to the flames, the thing or the place or the person mysteriously designated by "him" or "it." This is all we have any right to formulate. But perhaps there is no reason to go looking for a solution: the pseudoprophet, in a philological mood, may quite simply have picked out, from among the collection of flamens suggested by Varro or Macrobe, the word that provided both a rich and an easy rhyme with "Quirinal."

When I had finished reading, Espopondie remarked: "You see, Nostradamus did not hesitate to invent, or at least inflate, a prophecy by transposing a chapter from Titus-Livy relating to the origins of Rome into the future of the Church. His erudition provided him with inspiration."

"So he's an impostor?"

"Maybe. Even probably, in this case. But not necessarily. If, in his famous neurons, there were processes going on that were as complex as those producing the quatrain about Varennes, it is possible to think that, from time to time, the fantastic wealth of readings fermenting there might mix a bit of their honey with the flood of the future flowing into them."

I was listening distractedly, because for a few minutes now I had been thinking about something else. I was sure I had come upon another quatrain in the *Centuries* that also recalled, and was even more like, Numa's *inauguratio*. I asked Espopondie to give me a moment to find it in my copy of Le Pelletier.

First I came upon this one, 2.99, which establishes at least that Nostradamus was interested in another detail of augural doctrine, which interpreted auspices differently according to whether they appeared on *ager Romanus* [Roman land] or in four other sorts of *agri*: *Gabinus, peregrinus, hosticus, incertus* [lands: Gabinian, foreign, enemy, undetermined]:

> *Terroir Romain qu'interpretoit augure*
> *Par gent Gauloise par trop sera vexe.*
>
> (The Roman country that the augur interpreted
> By Gallic people shall be far too troubled.)

"Roman country" is a good translation, unfortunately forgotten by our contemporaries, of *ager Romanus*. But I was almost certain that there was a better example. It was not long before I located quatrain 5.6, which, in fact, reproduces the same gestures as those of the augur in Numa's inauguration. And this time the augur is named:

> *Au Roy l'Augur sur le chef la main mettre*
> *Viendra prier pour la paix Italique:*
> *A la main gauche viendra changer le sceptre,*
> *De Roy viendra Empereur pacifique.*
>
> (The augur shall come to place his hand on the king's head
> And shall pray for the peace of Italy:
> Shall come change the sceptre to the left hand
> From king shall become a peaceable emperor.)

This is how I interpreted it:

"You can easily identify the sort of event alluded to by Nostradamus: the promotion of a king who is already king to emperor. That was the old rule of the Holy Roman Empire, and that is what Bismarck wanted to reproduce in 1871 in the Hall of Mirrors for the benefit of his boss, the king of Prussia. This is an event that is plausible in itself and that has been repeated three or four times every century since the Middle Ages. But onto it the prophet has conscientiously and anachronistically transposed this ceremony—the one that, in Titus-Livy, made Numa, a mere private individual, into the successor of Romulus. Like his Roman colleague, the 'augur' he describes places a hand, probably his right hand, on the head of the king who is going to become emperor. But to do this, he must first free this right hand, which initially was holding the bent stick, the lituus. Like his Roman colleague he therefore passes this lituus, interpreted as a 'scepter,' from his right to his left hand. Only then can he consult (what God??), and there you have the king transformed into the emperor and, more precisely—to be faithful to the classical type represented by Numa, who wanted to be the antithesis of the warlike Romulus and during whose reign Rome did not know the meaning of war—into a 'peaceable emperor.'"

Espopondie was extremely happy with the way I had extended the analysis.

"You are more clever than I. But our conclusions are in agreement: with Nostradamus, the philologist sometimes provided some cheap relief for the seer. And Titus-Livy was probably not alone in having brought in fresh supplies. You can recommend to his disciples that they reread the old chronicles as well as Joinville, Villehardouin, and Commines. Our plunderer must not have been ignorant of them."

That was the last occasion we had for speaking of an author who, I had just begun to realize, had held a position I would not have expected in our friend's thought.

Spring went by. My work as reader-cremator came to an end. In June, provided with a grant from the École des Langues Orientales, I went to Czechoslovakia and traveled around that magnificent and varied country, daydreaming my way through the battlefields: Austerlitz, honest and bare, classical; Sadova, formidable and wooded, romantic. Espopondie, in his nice way, grew impatient, writing me that if I wanted to see him alive again I should not dally in Bohemia. In fact, at the beginning of August I received the unpleasant telegram: he had been struck down one morning as he was getting up, the aorta having drained into his trachea. I just had time to get to Paris, where I found the coffin closed. Along with a few Orientalists, I accompanied him to the cemetery. I was the only one of our group. De Momordy had already assumed his post, not with the Turks, as he had hoped, but in Madrid, and Charles Leslucas was spending the summer in Lorraine, where he was born. Upon my arrival, the secretary gave me an envelope with my name on it, entrusted to him by Espondie. Within it, without a word accompanying them, were two large photographs: one of the person who for ten years had been both his joy and a source of concern; the other of a passing fancy, but a very pretty one. No doubt he had found them after I left. Or had he hidden them from me? Without waiting for him to be in the ground I did my duty, at the fireplace.

"We Owe a Cock to Asclepius . . ."

A Divertissement on the Last Words of Socrates

For François Toussaint,
in memory of Gustave Charles Toussaint
and Roger Caillois

I

Among the many vivid memories I still have of your father, one, particularly, has waited almost fifty years to reach some sort of conclusion within me—a conclusion that was unexpected, and no doubt fortunate. I do not know exactly where I am as I write you, but I am eager to let you in on the secret.

This was at the very beginning of our relationship. You were fifteen years old and your father was already an old man, formerly a high-ranking magistrate for the overseas territories. He always spent his vacations traveling around the world, and you, for the first time, were brought along on one of his summer excursions, this time a three-week cruise on the comfortable ship *La Fayette*, which was to sail from Scotland to the Faeroe Islands, then from Iceland to Greenland, then sail along the ice pack as far as Spitzberg, and make the classic descent via the Norwegian fjords, back down to Le Havre. I was a member of the party, my soul black and blue from the last sentimental cataclysm of my life—or at least I thought it was the last—and I had brought with me one of my best students from Paris, quite a young man, with hundreds of favorable signs promising the fine future that was later confirmed in reality. He had been the witness of, and somewhat my confidant during, my interior upheavals. I felt strong ties with your father very quickly, instantly liking him and soon admiring him greatly. He fascinated me. He was able to read a Tibetan epic in the original just as well as a tragedy by Aeschylus. He was elegantly agnostic and did not conceal his indulgent fondness for the ways in which Buddhism—all Buddhisms—imagined the world.

We used to take our meals at the same table, and several times a day, in our deck chairs or leaning on the rail, we talked about everything and nothing. One afternoon our ship passed close by Jan Mayen, a dream island miraculously roused from its perpetual fog for a few hours, and I remarked to your father that this, perhaps, was where our great-uncles, the ancient Irish, had situated the place to which their dead would withdraw for their sojourn in the West, beyond the ocean. Reminiscing, daydreaming, passing from the *Voyage of Bran* to the Elysian fields in the *Phaedo*, we wound up discussing the last day of Socrates and the sublime and futile talk with which he filled the most difficult hours of all. Since my earliest youth his *ultima verba* had delighted me: "Crito, we owe a cock to Asclepius, pay the debt and do not forget!" I repeated them in French and in Greek, and I saw a sort of question in your father's mischievous eyes. "What do you understand by that?" he seemed to be saying. Naively, I said that my sense of it was that Socrates, seeing himself delivered from this disease only curable by death, which for a philosopher is life in this world, was entrusting to his friends the task of showing his gratitude to the god who was the master of healing.

"No, no, my friend," your father said, so sharply that it took me by surprise. "No. Socrates was no Buddhist. Life for him was a time of trials and suffering, but also of possibilities and joy. Certainly not a condition of illness! Rather a moral gymnasium where the wise man makes himself the master of the muscles of his soul, a place he then leaves without regret, the way a champion retires, either for eternal dreamless sleep or going in complete tranquillity to the Elysian fields, where, together with great men made famous by their swords, their words, or their minds, he will pursue the thoughts begun in the midst of all our tumult. No, for him, this world was not *duhkha*—

pure misfortune—nor was death a cure. Everything he taught, far from detaching young people from life, prepared them to live it truly."

Being corrected this way had a strong effect on me, like many things your father said in the course of those tightly packed days, and it made a deep impression philologically, if one may describe it that way. Certainly it continues to guard me against the hasty assimilations that wreak so much havoc in the history of ideas. Less tolerant than your father, I tended, from that point on, to put minds into two categories: those who believed that the cock in the *Phaedo* was the price to pay for the passage from the illness of life to the health of death (as I, in the wake of many others, had thought), and those who, like your father and—after this moment at Jan Mayen—me, did not believe this. Only the minds of the second group were sound. I even became surprisingly touchy on the subject: a student or philosopher or editor had only to commit this misinterpretation to fall in my esteem. So there were many people, even those bearing great names, who became dwarfs in my sight.

Nearly half a century has gone by since our cruise. How many times, cleansed of my youthful error and well armed against a repeat offense, have I tried to understand the message of the philosopher tipsy with hemlock! I soon learned, of course, that I was not alone, but that a thick and multiplying bibliography, like shellfish riding on flotsam, covered this "estremo voto di Socrates," this "Socrates' debt to Asclepius," these "last words of Socrates" or "Sokrates siøste ord." Nothing of what I had read had ever satisfied me. A number of writers put an end to the question by assuming that Socrates, with his dying breath, had thought of something completely different than the act he was completing. Wilamowitz, with a long parade of exegetes both before and after him, assumes that Socrates suddenly remembers a vow made to Asclepius for a disease of which there is no mention in the chronicle—a debt he has forgotten to settle. According to others, Socrates, an altruist to the very end, wanted to offer the cock for the restored health of a friend. And which friend? Plato himself!

Others have thought that Socrates was making fun of people. Still others would have it that Socrates, to confuse those who accused him of impiety, invented a debt to an altogether minor god. Someone found it natural that Socrates would be delirious as the poison, after having overcome his limbs, attacked his brain. One optimist assumed that Socrates simply wanted to express his gratitude to the god who had kept him in good health for so long. Is there any sense in dragging out this anthology of inventiveness? I resigned myself to not understanding.

The other day, or else maybe today, just a few hours ago, I do not know, I spent the heat of the afternoon in the pleasant summer sun in a corner of my garden, which lies at the foot of the unfortunately militarized heights through which the Vexin plateau has surrendered to the Seine's erosion. That morning I had had a little dizzy spell that worried my family, although it went away quickly, so I thought it best to stay in a lawn chair reading or dozing. As I settled myself down there, my dear François, I thought hard and long of your father, feeling some jealousy for the wonderful way he died. Two years after our cruise along the ice fields, two years before the Second World War, he too stretched out in a deck chair in the garden of your villa in Paramé, looking out toward the sea, and began reading the little copy of *De rerum natura* that he always carried in his pocket. Probably so he could give more thought to a beautiful passage, he lay the book on his right knee, his index finger between two pages, and closed his eyes. He never opened them again and the book never fell. Toward evening a lovely insect fluttered familiarly around him on wings of fire, as if conveying his farewell to you.

There on my lawn chair I was musing over this wonderful departure, with just the vaguest hint of wishfulness deep in my soul. There are not many books in my summer cottage, and I had taken with me, for no particular reason, a volume of poems by Lamartine. At the very end of it there are some fragments of "The Death of Socrates" that, I think, I had not reread since my youth. I stumbled upon the outrageous lines:

(this) said, he closed his eyes for the last time
And stayed for moments with no breath or voice.
A false ray of life strayed occasionally by
And lit his pale forehead with dying purple.
Thus, on a pure late autumn evening
When the sun has already left the horizon,
A forgotten ray frees itself from the shadows
To color in passing the golden flanks of a cloud.
Finally he seemed to breathe more freely,
And letting his sweet smile stray across his features:
"To the liberating gods," he said, "make sacrifice!
They have cured me!"—"Of what?" said Cebes.—
"Of life!"
Then a light sigh spilled from his lips,
As gentle as the flight of a bee from Hybla.
Was it? . . . I know not; but, filled with the dittany of
holy healing
We felt as if we had within us some second soul.

It was not holy healing dittany that fell into my soul, but sharp irritation, surprisingly sharp, as if my soul had been wounded in some sensitive spot: Asclepius spirited away among "liberating gods," this death curing an incurable disease—life! Everything your father had said against this misinterpretation as we stood before the snows of Jan Mayen surged in, converging so powerfully that, less fortunate than your father, I had no time to set the book on my left knee. It dropped to the ground. I felt a slight jolt beneath my diaphragm and I was asleep.

Strange sleep! I instantly awoke, feeling fine, in a completely different garden, or rather in a charming grove where human forms conversed soundlessly in small groups. Were they recognizable? Probably, but I knew only a few. But one at least came to me with his arms wide open, as if for an embrace. It was your father, welcoming me to this strange Inferno!

"My friend, my friend," he said to me, in a voice recalling his own, "I noticed your fit of anger just now and I beg you to forgive me. I provoked it because I was the one who steered your hand toward that fool Lamartine. Calm down. Impulses of the heart are not appreciated here. When I feel you have yourself under control I shall take you to see one among us who, I believe, has given much thought to what disturbs both you and me, and who, for a long time, would have been only too happy to unlock its meaning for us. He has been waiting for you to join us, no doubt, before enlightening us.

"Here," your father added, as he led me to the oracle, "we keep our personalities but not our persons. We no longer have any self-love; we no longer have our blinders. All we care about is seeking a truth, and we are no less happy when this comes on the breath of another than when it is the result of our own thoughts. We speak the same language, and I often have the impression that we are all simply the undifferentiated cells of one great brain. Ah, if the living could only adapt themselves with such machinery!" He sighed and then went on. "But really, don't the dialogues of Plato already provide the model for this? It's a pity that most of the philosophers who have come after him have preferred to go in circles, each one in his brilliant solitude."

He probably saw how perplexed I was.

"It's not easy for me to make the way we communicate clear to you," he went on. "Do we speak? Do we intertwine or intermix our thoughts without articulating them? It must be something else, something that defies the words that, nonetheless, we continue to use when they are called for. But this evening—for we live in a perpetual and luminous eventide, like that unforgettable sky fifty years ago, with the peaks of Jan Mayen against it—this evening we shall speak, as we always do with new arrivals, the way you are accustomed to communicating, but with no vanity or passion, with no personal animation: too much heat would be painful for us."

"Sir," I said. "Because it is something Socrates said that we do not understand, why not go ask the philosopher himself? Isn't he somewhere in your anthropological garden?"

"My friend, he is here, in fact, and with a bit of effort, we can already see him. But he won't help you. Not that we have been growing older, as the living do, but we never stop maturing, and the eldest among us, while forgetting nothing, achieve such simplicity and limpidity of mind that they no longer recognize problems and communicate only with smiles. No, I know the one to take you to. But at his side he will surely have his other half, who, even here where we live, remains what he was on earth, *dimidium animae* [half of (his) soul]. They are always together, one asking questions and the other answering, carefully weighing everything, the greatest or the least of matters. They are so full of these old writings that they will certainly open a Socratic dialogue in your presence. You will hardly have to participate in it except by brief signs of approval or, if you insist, with objections that are almost as brief. To identify you, shall we translate our names into Athenian Greek? You will be Brizopyrinos and I will be Panagios."

"Yes, I would like that," I replied. "But I hope we will seldom need to delight the ghost of Aristophanes with these names."

"Don't worry, that troublemaker is not among us."

We were already standing before two forms, still young, whom I thought I recognized, and even recognized several times over because they reminded me of more than one philosopher whom the gods loved too much to lend to the earth for long.

"Let's say their names are Kossyphidios and Gephyrios. But you need only call them 'master' or 'sir.' Or, if you really do recognize them, 'my friend.'"

Kossyphidios was already waving his transparent hand to me in greeting.

"I know the problem that interests you, sir," he said. "I know it all the better because formerly, in the cave, it annoyed me, and even here I have put in a great deal of time—if that word has any meaning—persuading myself that I have solved it. I have in fact perhaps resolved it, even though our brother Gephyrios is not entirely convinced. Let me thank you for providing me a chance to go back and pick up this debate once again."

Gephyrios amiably shrugged his transparent shoulders.

KOSSYPHIDIOS: "First, let us understand this apparently simple text: ῏Ω Κρίτων, τῷ 'Ασκληπιῷ ὀφείλομεν ἀλεκτρῦονα, ἀλλὰ ἀπόδοτε καὶ μὴ ἀμελήσητε, 'O Crito, we owe a cock to Asclepius, pay the debt and do not forget!' Perhaps in our lifetimes we were not sufficiently respectful of philology, and this frequently was an impediment to our interpretations. Here, separated from our works, we would willingly espouse it if Mercury had not already done so. In any event, we acknowledge its rights, we savor its charms. Let us make it, therefore, our first principle as we confront the last message from Socrates!"

After a brief moment of contemplation he went on: "Yes, so much grammar in these few words! I see, whether they are straightforward or disguised, two numbers and three persons: 'O Crito' is a singular addressed to a singular, intimate 'you,' and not the plural 'you'; thus it is a vocative indicating a second person. 'We owe,' 'pay,' and 'do not forget' are first-person and then (twice) second-person plurals. How are these dramatis personae linked? And above all, what precisely is included in these plural forms? Each form considered as itself is ambiguous. Is 'we' restrictive or extensive? Is it 'we, that is you, Crito whom I have just addressed, and I,' or is it 'me, you, and them, everyone here present?' And 'you,' is this what it seems—'you, you who are here present'? Or indeed—because I don't want to exclude anything in advance, not even the idea that this 'you' may be an elegant turn of phrase from a philosopher breathing his last—'you, that is, you whom suddenly I am entrusting with a great responsibility, you, one of the yet living mortals, representative of all your fellow men, from whom I already grow more distant.'"

GEPHYRIOS: "Not all of your explanations are equally plausible. Regarding the 'we': if it were extensive, coextensive with those in attendance, if Socrates had in mind that the debt was the equal responsibility of all those friends who were present, why separately specify 'Crito' in the vocative? Doesn't this individual request imply that Crito is the principal, if not the only, one involved, along with Socrates, in the verb introduced by this vocative?"

Your father, Panagios, now felt it would be polite to step in. "That is not certain. Crito, who was his lifelong friend and was as weighed down by the years as Socrates, usually acted as his agent. He was the one, right at the beginning of the *Phaedo*, whom Socrates asked to send away anybody who might weep too loudly, the women, and the children; then, once again, as evening approached, he was the one sent by Socrates to tell the servant of the Eleven that it was time for the hemlock."

KOSSYPHIDIOS: "The situation is no longer the same at the very end of the *Phaedo*. Socrates is not giving Crito a task, something to say or do right away, or something concerning outsiders, if one may call them that—the wife or the jailer. He is reminding him of a duty. If 'we' contained 'me, you, and them' on equal terms, would he not have said, with all the precision that fit these circumstances—the final words of a vast work—'O my friends'? What reason could he have had to single out Crito from the group in the presence of everyone, if every member of that group shared equally in the duty?"

GEPHYRIOS: "Indeed, but there are two plurals, one a first-person plural and then, immediately thereafter, the pair of second-person plurals: 'We owe . . . pay the debt and do not forget.' Does this not oblige us to include within these two plurals the same individuals, with the exception of Socrates himself, who—although living at the moment the debt was contracted, would be dead at the moment when it would be paid—is naturally present in 'we' and excluded from 'you'? As for your supposition that there is an emphatic, royal plural applied to Crito alone, it has no basis. As you say, Socrates is not concerned with style with his last breath; he wants to be understood without ambiguity. So, if this plural 'you' is indeed 'you and them,' isn't it natural, through contagion, to understand the preceding 'we' as 'me, you, and them, all of us'?"

KOSSYPHIDIOS: "What you say is true, but what I said is no less so. Let's split the difference. Perhaps Socrates does not address Crito merely as Crito but as the representative of the whole group, and by this delegation he places the whole group under obligation, with Crito a sort of choragus in this tragedy begun long ago and now coming to a close."

GEPHYRIOS: "That is not impossible. But I think the grammar has given us all it can. Let's not push it. Let's torture the words instead, the most important ones first, because the two imperatives at the end certainly harbor no secret or key. We are left with the beginning: 'We owe a cock to Asclepius.' The cock? It has never caused any difficulty, nor does it now. It is the chosen creature everywhere, even in Athens, for the sacrifice expected by Asclepius in thanksgiving—with the result that it all comes down to this: Why Asclepius?"

Here we stopped for a few moments—or were they centuries?—for a swallow of that subtle variety of orangeade they drink in the Elysian fields. It is to the nectar of gods what our shadows are to our bodies. Then Kossyphidios went on: "There is only one service rendered by Asclepius in the world of humankind. He deals only with those who are ill: if they spend a night sleeping in his sanctuary, they will receive in a dream the prescription that will cure them."

GEPHYRIOS: "In the case of Socrates, what illness and what prescription could this be?"

KOSSYPHIDIOS: "That, in fact, is the real question. But first, now that we have Asclepius restored to the center of the problem, we absolutely must go back and look at the grammar, the numbers and persons in these two little sentences. Who, what man or what men, were ill and became cured? 'We owe a cock': once again, who is 'we'? Socrates? Socrates and Crito? Socrates, Crito, and the others? The compromise that we arrived at just now would take shape as follows: 'Crito, we owe a cock to Asclepius in gratitude for the cure that you know about and that has concerned us as sick men, you and me, and also, behind you, our other friends."

GEPHYRIOS: "That would, in fact, justify the interaction of the verb forms. In any event, it seems out of the question that it is Socrates alone who has been cured, don't you think?"

KOSSYPHIDIOS: "That is the usual assumption, with the result that the explanations are lame. If it is only Socrates, we have no handle on it. Not to mention those who think that the great man's *sententia ultima* [final sentence] makes no sense, whether because he is rambling under the influence of poison or because he merely wishes to fling a posthumous denial at those who accused him of not honoring the city's gods. This assumes that it concerns the cure for some old disease not mentioned anywhere else but which he suddenly remembers, and that he then wants to pay what he owes. This is artificial. It has also been thought that Socrates is eager to thank Asclepius for a sort of 'cure in advance,' for having spared him the physical miseries of old age, which, given his age, were imminent. That is impossible. Asclepius is a technician; he only cures actual, stated ills. The service imputed to him here—provided before an illness, outside the illness—would come, rather, under the jurisdiction of some other god, such as Zeus or Apollo, or any other god who was the protector of this man or that. In the *Apology*, at least in that of Xenophon, Socrates, who was in fact delighted to escape old age's decline, is especially pleased to be leaving the world in perfect health, which really could be of no interest to Asclepius! It has more frequently been assumed that Socrates meant to suggest that death is the remedy for the disease of life itself, any human life.

"But this is contrary to everything he taught, which was directed toward putting life to good use. Although occasionally, in the *Phaedo* and elsewhere, he claims—making the most charming assumption—to be happy that he will be able to converse with the shades of great men in the Elysian fields and to put them to the test, following his obsessive habit of acting as a midwife, and although occasionally he says that, because the sleeping hours are the best part of life, the uninterrupted sleep with no awakening that death represents—according to the other, materialist hypothesis—can only be a good and desirable fate, he never presents life as a disease in itself or death as a 'liberation.' When the young Theban in the *Phaedo* curiously becomes involved in fantasies of reincarnation, Socrates does not follow him. The first of the four truths of his colleague in fine sophistry, Sakyamuni—'all is suffering'—is foreign to him. Does it become any more plausible if we reduce the range of the words by saying that he thanks Asclepius for having delivered him, not from life in general, but from this distressing portion of life that has gone by between the sentence and the hemlock? Once again, no: moral ordeals are not diseases, and, moreover, the attitude of Socrates throughout the *Apology*, the *Crito*, and the *Phaedo* demonstrates a serenity and refusal to dramatize that surprises his stricken friends. Except for the shackles that pinch his legs, from which he is happy to be set free at the beginning of the *Phaedo*, he does not complain about the prison regime. He has not suffered either physically or morally. He has eaten and slept in peace; he has even had pleasant visits. No, however we look at it, Socrates is not a 'sick man.'"

Your father spoke up once again. Had there not been infinity in his gaze and a strange modulation to his voice, I would have thought we were off Jan Mayen.

PANAGIOS: "I do not see, in fact, what other sort of disease, of νόσος, afflicting only Socrates, could have given rise to an intervention by Asclepius."

KOSSYPHIDIOS: "Therefore there is no choice, is there, except to fall back on the other interpretation: the disease and the cure affect Crito and Socrates as a couple in the foreground, with their friends in the background?"

GEPHYRIOS: "Inevitably."

KOSSYPHIDIOS: "As soon as Crito and Socrates are seen thus as a couple in the foreground, is it not natural to seek the disease and cure in the dialogue that Plato has named after the former, and in which the two alone are present?"

GEPHYRIOS: "That is not a bad idea."

KOSSYPHIDIOS: "And it is all the more natural because in this dialogue named for Crito, Crito does not present himself, or speak, or act—except as the delegate or the leader, if not of the entire group of Socrates' friends, at least of the most fortunate, the young Thebans themselves, who will reappear, playing an active and emotional role, in the *Phaedo*."

GEPHYRIOS: "Of course, but then we encounter two problems. First, because Socrates has not been ill, the sick man, the real sick man, must be Crito, or Crito and his constituents. Now, they appear to be just as healthy as Socrates! On the other hand, suppose they are 'sick.' How does Socrates—who isn't sick—fit into their relationship with the physician god, a relationship that is nonetheless so tight that he acknowledges that he is equally committed to the debt that they have contracted toward this god upon the occasion of their cure?"

KOSSYPHIDIOS: "You ask too many questions at once. I shall answer your first one. It is inaccurate to say that Crito, or Crito and his constituents, were not ill in the *Crito*. They were."

GEPHYRIOS: "I don't understand."

KOSSYPHIDIOS: "Let's take another look at the *Crito* from the beginning to the end. Or rather, let's take the beginning and the end.

"Crito comes into the prison at dawn and, as soon as Socrates awakens, after a brief controversy about whether the next day or the day after that is the day Socrates legally must die, Crito explains his project, his mission. Everything is ready; the favors are all paid for. Socrates can leave prison the next night and reach Thessaly, where one of Crito's friends will receive him as an honored guest. Every objection has been foreseen: the small conspiracy has gotten together a lot of money, part of which will be used for Socrates' escape and the rest later to bribe the informers and the judges of Athens if they prove too curious. There remains the question of the morality of the operation. How could this be debatable? Socrates is not guilty; his sentence is unjust; therefore he has the right to evade the hemlock—the right and even the duty, because he is not alone in the world. He has children and, especially, he has disciples, and his teaching, for all of Greece, for humanity, is an irreplaceable treasure . . . Socrates refuses, argues, proves his case. When he is finished he simply says:

"'Know that anything you can say against what seems just to me at this moment will be in vain. If, however, you think you are capable of making me change my mind, then speak.'

"Crito replies: 'No, Socrates, I have nothing to say.'

"And Socrates concludes: 'So, Crito, let it be and let us act in this way, because this is the way in which the god is leading us.'

"We don't know what happens next; the dialogue ends. Crito, when he left the prison, would certainly have called off the operation and let his friends know. At the beginning of the *Phaedo*, in Socrates' final hours, no one will reproach him for the decision that appalls them, making the most fragile among them cry."

GEPHYRIOS: "You have summarized very well what took place on the morning two days earlier. Crito's conversion is indeed striking. He, and his constituents through him, acknowledged that they were wrong and that, as always, Socrates had formulated and proved the sound proposition. But that, I think, is not what you are calling 'disease' and 'cure,' is it?"

KOSSYPHIDIOS: "Yes, my friend. This is how Socrates reasoned. Wrong opinion is to the soul what disease is to the body. This is even the doctrine, the postulate, if you will, of which he reminds Crito, to which he carefully makes Crito agree before undertaking to convince him. Crito was silly enough to tell him that if he did not get away from the Eleven, public opinion would condemn him and condemn his friends for not having made the sacrifices or run the risks that would allow his salvation."

Then Kossyphidios read from his memory as if it were a book, repeating Crito's final appeals:

"CRITO: 'For, in the end, either one should not have children or one should take a great deal of trouble with them to the very end, feeding them and raising them—whereas it seems to me you have made the less manly choice. Your choice should be that of a brave, good man, especially after you have spent your entire life asserting your attachment to virtue. The result is that I am ashamed for you and for us, your friends. I fear that people will think this whole affair has been conducted with a certain cowardice on our part. There was, first, the accusation brought before the tribunal, which did not have to happen; then there was the way the trial itself unfolded; and now this absurd ending to the play. We have shirked our duties, they will say, out of cowardice, out of spinelessness; we no more saved you than you saved yourself, when it was quite possible if only we had been willing to make a bit of effort. Consider, therefore, in addition to the evil itself, the extent to which this would be shameful both for yourself and for us.'

"'The opinion of the majority, those who are ignorant, does not matter much,' Socrates replied. Only the opinion of wise men counts for the health of the body or that of the soul:

"SOCRATES: 'Should the man who is a serious gymnast attach any importance to the compliments or criticisms or opinions of just anybody, or only the opinion of one man who is either a doctor or a trainer?'

"CRITO: 'Only to the opinion of that one.'

"SOCRATES: 'So he should fear the blame and welcome the praise only of that one, not of the multitude?'

"CRITO: 'Of course.'

"SOCRATES: 'If he disobeys that one, if—only valuing the words of the multitude, of those who know nothing about it—he scorns that man's opinion and praise, will this not result in harm for him?'

"CRITO: 'Inevitably.'

"SOCRATES: 'What harm is at stake? Where is it felt? What part of the one who disobeys is affected?'

"CRITO: 'His body, obviously, because it is his body that is damaged.'

"SOCRATES: 'You are right. In short, without losing ourselves in details, let's say that the same is true for everything: where things that are just and unjust, beautiful and ugly, good and bad are concerned —the things we are now deliberating—should we follow the opinion of the many and fear it, or only that of the man, if he exists, who has knowledge of these things and whom we must respect and fear more than all the others together? So if we do not follow his opinion we shall harm and corrupt (διαφθεροῦμεν καὶ λωϐησόμεθα) the part of us that is improved by what is just and destroyed by what is unjust? Is that not important?'

"CRITO: 'Yes, Socrates, I believe that is important.'

"SOCRATES: 'Well, if, persuaded by the opinion of those ignorant in the matter, we destroy that part of us that is improved by things that are healthy (ὑγιεινοῦ) and is damaged by things causing disease (νοσώδους), can we live following this destruction? We are talking about the body here, of course.'

"CRITO: 'I agree.'

"SOCRATES: 'Can we live with a body that is sick and damaged?'

"CRITO: 'Certainly not.'

"SOCRATES: 'But then, can we live when the other part, that which is damaged by the unjust and strengthened by the just, is harmed? Or do we regard that other part of ourselves, whatever it is, that is concerned with the just and the unjust as of lesser value?'

"CRITO: 'Not at all.'

"SOCRATES: 'More valuable, on the contrary?'

"CRITO: 'Far more.'

"SOCRATES: 'We should not then be so worried, my friend, about what most people will say, but only about what the one alone who understands what is just and what is unjust will say—he alone, and through him the truth itself. To conclude this first point, the advice you are giving me is not right because it assumes that we have to be concerned with the opinion of the many when it is a question of justice, virtue, good, and their opposites.'"

KOSSYPHIDIOS: "The disease that destroys the body is thus the twin sister of the false opinion that corrupts the soul. Physical illness cannot be treated by the crowd of ignorant men, but by a specialist alone, the man dedicated to Asclepius, the medical doctor; false opinion, which most often comes from unthinking submission to the opinion of the many, cannot be corrected except by enlightened, philosophical judgment, based on sure principles. It is really a matter of reestablishing the equilibrium of the mind, making it *phronimos*—which you may translate however you wish: healthy, wise, well-ordered; it's all the same thing. Socrates, moreover, specified the dividing line at the beginning of his refutation, just before comparing the care of the body to that of the soul, and he uttered the two words clarifying everything:

"SOCRATES: 'Are we not right to say that we should not prize all of men's opinions, but only some and not others, those of certain men and not those of certain others? What do you say to this? Is this not the right way to put it?'

"CRITO: 'It is.'

"SOCRATES: 'And the opinions that are right are those of *phronimoi*; the wrong ones are those of *aphrones*. In other words, the former are the opinions of minds that function soundly and the latter are those of minds that function poorly?'

"CRITO: 'How can one argue with this?'

"In short," Kossyphidios went on, "the *aphrôn* is one who is 'mind-sick.' The philosopher's task, the mission conferred upon him by the god of Delphi, whose spirit would frequently remind him of it and not allow him to keep silent, was to transform *aphrones* into *phronimoi*—in short, to heal them."

GEPHYRIOS: "Yes, I understand where you are taking us. The healing that earns the cock for Asclepius is the healing of Crito himself: Socrates, the doctor of thought, leads his old friend from an idea that is brilliant but insane to one that is sound; Crito becomes convinced, leaving behind the many, along with the error of things they consider obvious, and he joins those who support the laws. He is healed. However, I have two problems with this; here is the first.

"The *aphrôn*, in all of the master's explanations, is indeed a sort of sick person: that comes out in the extended parallel between the body, which is fought over by the 'unhealthy' and the 'healthy,' νοσωδές and ὑγιεινόν, and the mind, which is either disordered or in good order, *aphrôn* and *phronimos*. However, nowhere does Socrates make any claim to *healing*; he merely wants to *convince* his interlocutor. The 'treatment' you speak of is purely intellectual. Socrates does not use, even once, the word νόσος 'disease,' about the soul. Throughout the entire exposition the word appears only one time, and it is on the other panel of the diptych, concerning the body. It is, therefore, only a comparison, an image, with respect to the soul. Now, when Homer compares a hero to a lion he does not identify him with the lion; he just points to some resemblance in their behavior. Similarly here, the *aphrôn* is only compared to someone who is ill and erroneous opinion to a disease. Do 'error cleared up dialectically' and 'reason restored through proof' fall under the jurisdiction of Asclepius—who, moreover, is also not mentioned anywhere in the *Crito*?"

KOSSYPHIDIOS: "My friend, a well-chosen comparison, in the logic of Socrates, is the equivalent of reason. And then, despite appearances, despite the calm of the dialogue, this is about something more than an opinion. It is about a course of action, a decision—and a decision that is imminent, whose urgency the two partners emphasize. As he concludes his appeal, which seems so reasonable, Crito presses Socrates:

"CRITO: 'Take counsel, then. Or rather, it is no longer the moment to take counsel, but to have done so. There is only one conceivable decision, because it is necessary for everything to be accomplished by nightfall. If we delay, nothing will be possible; we shall no longer be able to do anything. Anyhow, trust me, Socrates. Do not do what must not be done.'

"Socrates, in turn, when he has completed his refutation and made Crito give in, concludes on a peremptory note:

"SOCRATES: 'Let it be and let us act, πράττωμεν, in the way I say, because this is the way in which the god is leading us.'

"Consequently, this debate is neither rhetorical nor speculative; it is dramatic, and with what stakes! Either, according to the right that every man has as his natural recourse against injustice, Socrates will live, or Socrates will die because he conforms to the laws even when they are unjustly employed by the legitimate authority."

GEPHYRIOS: "You are probably right, but I would have liked for Socrates to say to Crito in a straightforward manner: 'You are ill; let yourself be cared for and healed.'"

KOSSYPHIDIOS: "Are you aware that the debate pitting Socrates against Crito, despite the newness of its method, was magnificently settled about thirty-five years earlier in Sophocles' most famous tragedy? Creon, who had begun his government so well, made the gravest decision: he forbade any citizen, on pain of death, to provide burial for Creon's nephew, who had dared take up arms against his country. His niece, Antigone, the sister of the dead man, in the name of unwritten laws, violated this *kêrygma*, this prohibition promulgated by the legitimate authority, and she paid final respects to Polyneices. Creon immediately sent her to her prison-tomb. 'One of us has lost his mind,' she said to him in vain. And later: 'If you think I have done things that are mad, perhaps it is a madman who accuses me of madness.' He persisted in his intention. But suddenly, too late, the seer appeared—old, blind Tiresias, who had foretold all the misfortunes of Thebes since the birth of Oedipus:

"TIRESIAS: 'Think, child,' he said to King Creon. 'To err is something all men do. But when a man has made a mistake, he regains his wisdom and happiness if he heals (ἀκεῖται) the evil into which he has fallen and does not prove to be intractable . . . Yield to the dead therefore; do not hound the one who already is no more: where is the courage in killing a dead man a second time?'

"Creon was set in his mind and began to be abusive.

"CREON: 'No, you will not bury him in a tomb even if Zeus's eagles bear off to his throne the shreds of the body they prey upon! No, not even fear of this pollution will make me allow him to be buried; besides, I know that no man has the power to pollute the gods.'

"Then remember the verbal fencing that follows, which the specialists in the cave call stichomythia: Tiresias reminds the stubborn man that *euboulia*, the ability to hold sound, good counsel, is worth more than all wealth. Creon replies ironically:

"CREON: 'Yes, and bad reasoning, μὴ φρόνειν, is the worst thing of all, βλάβη.'

"TIRESIAS: 'And yet you are filled with this disease, Ταύτης τῆς νόσου!'

"Now look: will the imminent misfortunes already predicted for Thebes by the omens have resulted from the stubbornness of Creon, who is the author and upholder of a law that is, if one may say so, sacrilegious but legal, a law he was entitled to proclaim, κήρυγμα? Or will misfortune be kept at bay? That is, will he consent actually to do what his blindness has the illusion of doing, φρονεῖν: 'think well,' 'be wise'? Will he acknowledge the primacy of the unwritten law that Antigone was already using to oppose him? Now, this error in judgment, with its extremely grave consequences, is truly a disease of the mind, a νόσος. In short, Tiresias, before the palace at Thebes, is to Creon what Socrates, on his prison bed, is to Crito. But both the course of the debate and its results are reversed: the *aphrôn* wins out over the φρόνιμος; official law wins out over natural law—until the moment when Creon, his son threatened by a final prophecy of the seer, plunges headlong into the opposite opinion, through fear and not through conversion. Besides, it is too late: his son, Antigone's fiancé, has run himself through with his own sword, Antigone is hanging in her prison-tomb, and Creon's wife has stabbed herself to death. Sophocles, through the mouth of Tiresias, has pronounced the word νόσος to describe a wrong opinion generating reprehensible decisions. Do we agree on that?"

GEPHYRIOS: "Of course, but Sophocles is a pure poet. He is able to simplify or magnify things."

KOSSYPHIDIOS: "Would you prefer a philosopher-poet? Someone even slightly sophistic? A contemporary of Socrates? There is Euripides, who recounts how Agamemnon at Aulis resigned himself at first to sacrificing his daughter on the altar of cruel Artemis in order to obtain fair winds so he could dispatch the army and the fleet entrusted to his command. It was his duty to lead them to the city that was guilty of the rape of Helen, the wife of his brother, Menelaus.

But he goes back on this decision: father wins out over generalissimo, nature over institution. Consequently he must face Menelaus, who argues in favor of the national duty of the king of Greece and the professional duty of the generalissimo. Against this brother, Agamemnon sets natural law, his duty as a father:

"MENELAUS: 'How then will you prove to me that you are my brother?'

"AGEMEMNON: 'By wishing to think soundly with you, in a healthy manner (συνσωφρονεῖν), and by not being sick with you (συννοσεῖν)!'

"And, because Menelaus takes as cover the unanimous opinion of the army—that is, what Socrates in the *Crito* refers to as 'the many,' this mass whose opinion cannot be set against that of the wise man—Agamemnon sums up the argument in one line:

"'Greece is ill with you (σὺν σοὶ . . . νοσεῖ) through the will of some god.'

Socrates, therefore, did not invent this opposition between the 'sound thinking' that makes up the health of the mind and the disordered judgment that is its disease. Although he did not pronounce the word νοσωδές, 'unhealthy,' except as part of a comparison and regarding the body, it is nonetheless certainly the basis of his argument, and Crito understands it in this manner."

GEPHYRIOS: "Let's just say it, then: someone who errs in his opinions is what, in the cave, we used to call a person with mental illness? All right. But this is precisely where my second problem comes in—even two new problems.

"Whatever we said, it concerned a disease and a cure of a very specific sort. You yourself have just made the point that the *Crito* does not portray an attack of madness the therapy for which is electroshock. Calmly and lucidly, Crito formulates statements that are erroneous, and Socrates demonstrates his errors to him. Crito is convinced. If Asclepius has to intervene in cases that are as purely intellectual as this one he must be extremely busy, starting with kindergarten and in careers of all sorts. As far as every schoolboy, student, 'teacher,' and 'researcher'—as we call them today—is concerned, none of us has evolved except by correcting within himself, alone or with others, innumerable errors of judgment.

"And here is my second problem. It is natural for the 'sick man' or 'sick men,' Crito and his friends, to express their gratitude to Asclepius, the god of healing. But Socrates? Throughout the affair he has never erred. Is it customary for the doctor to share in his client's debt to the god? At the most he is able to ascertain that the cure has had a good effect, and to deliver a certificate of cure and good health for every useful purpose, religious or otherwise. So why the 'we': 'O Crito, *we* owe a cock to Asclepius'?"

KOSSYPHIDIOS: "Those are two very different questions; however, they can be resolved at the same time. But have we not resolved the first already, in fact? Never mind; some nails you have to pound in twenty times. As far as Asclepius's competence is concerned, Crito's disease and cure are not just some philosophical vagary, any more than are those of Creon. This is not an intellectual game: in Creon's case, because he was not cured in time, Antigone, Haemon, and Eurydice die wrongfully; in Crito's case, Socrates, who is more convincing than Tiresias, manages to confirm by his death what he has taught throughout his life. Therefore, although the disease and the cure are intellectual, the stakes and the results are not. Perhaps that is why Asclepius intervened—because you are forgetting that, in fact, he did intervene, just the way he usually does. Socrates was not mistaken, nor, probably, was Crito!"

GEPHYRIOS: "How is that?"

KOSSYPHIDIOS: "Let's go back to the *Crito* once again, at the very beginning, in the opening scene, which is so wonderfully simple. The visitor is there as the prisoner awakens:

"SOCRATES: 'Why did you come so early in the morning, Crito? Or is it not very early?'

"CRITO: 'Yes, it is, in fact.'

"SOCRATES: 'Exactly what time is it?'

"CRITO: 'Just barely dawn.'

"SOCRATES: 'I am surprised that the prison warden was willing to let you in.'

"CRITO: 'We are used to each other now and, besides, I have given him a few things.'

"SOCRATES: 'Did you just arrive or have you been here for a long time?'

"CRITO: 'For a rather long time.'

"SOCRATES: 'So why didn't you wake me right away, rather than sitting here beside me, saying nothing?'

"CRITO: 'Ah, by Zeus, no, Socrates! I myself would not want to miss my sleep at such a distressing time. So I stayed here for quite a while contemplating your sleep, which was so peaceful. To let you enjoy it as much as possible, I was careful not to wake you. I have, of course, envied your character many times during the course of your life, but now I admire it especially, seeing you bear your misfortune so easily and with such tranquillity.'

"SOCRATES: 'Come now, Crito, how unseemly it would be if, at my age, I complained about the fact that I must die "so soon"!'

"CRITO: 'Yes, but, Socrates, many others of your age become caught up in similar misfortunes, and age does not prevent their crying out against their fate.'

"Socrates cut short this lighthearted conversation, and Crito explained the present situation to him. The sacred ship returning from Delos had already reached port at Cape Sunium on the tip of Greece. It would therefore drop anchor in Piraeus before evening and, as death sentences—suspended during the course of the voyage—would be put into effect on the day following the end of this period of purity, tomorrow was the day on which the hemlock would be administered. Socrates interrupted:

"SOCRATES: 'May it be for the best! If this be the will of the gods, so be it! I do not think, however, that this will happen tomorrow.'

"CRITO: 'What indications of this do you have?'

"SOCRATES: 'I shall tell you. It is the day after the ship arrives that I must die, is it not?'

"CRITO: 'That is what those in charge say, at least.'

"SOCRATES: 'Well, I think that the boat will not return today, but rather tomorrow, and the basis of this feeling is a certain dream I had this very night, a few moments ago. It seems you were entirely right not to wake me!'

"CRITO: 'And what was the dream?'

"SOCRATES: 'I thought a beautiful and majestic woman all dressed in white came toward me, called me, and said "Socrates, in three days you can arrive in fertile Phthia."'

"CRITO: 'What a strange dream!'

"SOCRATES: 'It seems clear enough to me, at least, Crito.'

"CRITO: 'Yes, all too clear! But, dear Socrates, believe me, let me save you.'

"His arguments poured forth; he had contemplated them for a long time, and Socrates listened patiently. But in fact the cards were on the table. Socrates believed in the meaningfulness of dreams, as did Crito. 'Clear,' said one, and the other went further: 'Too clear'—as if he knew he had already lost the debate. Homer's line is slightly changed, but its relationship with Socrates' situation is obvious.

"In the third canto of the *Iliad*, Agamemnon's three ambassadors—Ulysses, the man of a thousand possibilities, Phoenix, the elderly mentor, and the warrior, Ajax—are in Achilles' tent, where they are attempting to bend his will. He should accept the reparation and compensation offered him by the king of kings; he should forgive him the offense committed in the first canto and return to the battle in which the Greeks are near surrender. Achilles, impervious and unwavering, refuses and goes one step further: he, in his *maiestas* [majestic dignity], will quit the war and leave the army. 'Tomorrow,' he tells Ulysses, 'if you care to, you will be able to watch my vessels sailing on the fish-filled Hellespont, driven by eager oarsmen, and, provided the god of the seas grants us a good crossing, 'In three days I can be on the fertile soil of Phthia.'

"Socrates revises Homer slightly, transposing the verb to the second person. This is no longer a hope, a personal decision. This is prophecy, duly registered. Despite the potential mood of the verb, which ought to diminish their certainty, he and Crito both interpret it as a definite portent of the philosopher's return to his true country, the Elysian fields, either the world of ideas or the land beneath the cave—and a return on a particular date: the third day, that is, according to Greek and Latin calculations, the day after tomorrow."

Your father spoke up:

"If you will permit me this digression? With all due respect, the interpretation made by Socrates and Crito seems arbitrary, strained, as sometimes happens when one takes a quote out of context. In another sense, Socrates is in the same situation as Achilles: he has been unjustly treated by a temporal authority. And what does Achilles decide? To desert, to leave the Greek army, to which, however, he is bound by at least some duty of solidarity. He would do this in good conscience if the 'Patrocles effect,' as the newspapers call it, did not require him to fulfill another and more immediate duty—vengeance. Therefore, if Socrates were to follow this epic example, he too would desert in good conscience. He would leave the thankless and unjust city and end his days in an exile where he knows perfectly well, despite what he says of it later, he would be made comfortable by his friends and his fame. And isn't the home that Crito has prepared for him in Thessaly where Phthia, Achilles' homeland, is also?"

KOSSYPHIDIOS: "Perhaps, but the fact is that, in prison, the two friends, with no hesitation, understood the line otherwise: 'In three days, you will have left the world of troubles, and you will be at home as Achilles was in Phthia.' Exegetes usually only pay attention to the date, the postponement indicated in the dream, the 'day after tomorrow' that Socrates opposes to Crito's 'tomorrow.' They forget the most important thing: the day after tomorrow or tomorrow, basically it makes little difference; in any case the woman in white is saying you are going to die, you must die. This is at the heart of the revelation, and at the same time, it is the solution to Crito's problem or, if you will, the 'remedy' for what Socrates' refutation and his own conversion will soon make us understand is his error, his 'disease.'"

GEPHYRIOS: "Again I think I see where you are taking us. But continue to be our guide."

KOSSYPHIDIOS: "I am not taking you anywhere. We are here. Divine decision has become mixed up in, or superimposed in advance on, the intellectual debate between Crito and Socrates. The dream, one obviously inspired or 'sent,' could only confirm Socrates in the decision he made as a philosopher, and, although nothing was said about this, it was 'too clear' and weakened Crito's resistance—if ever anyone can resist a skillful philosopher. In short, the game is split in two, and it takes up two floors of the great casino that is our world. The game has already been played, quickly and silently, in the invisible realm that communicates with our world only by oracles, signs, and dreams of premonition. It is also going to be played out, wordy and futile, on the earth, in prison, between two men. The truth of this can be seen in the last words given to Socrates in the *Crito*: they are not something a dialectician who has conquered his adversary would say, but the words of a pious man obeying a divine order. After Crito capitulates, he does not say, 'Stop arguing, let me do what I'm going to do, because you have acknowledged that I am right.' He says, 'Crito, let it be and let us act in the way I say, because this is the way in which the god is leading us'—and not just leading us, but leading us 'from beneath,' by intervening within us, if you will, through a sort of preestablished harmony that is easily explainable. Because Socrates is perfectly virtuous and 'knows' what is good, the prescription given by the god who sent the dream turned out to conform perfectly to the decision that his life as a philosopher and midwife could only have inspired in him."

GEPHYRIOS: "I know what you are going to say, but I want to look as if I'm helping you: why Asclepius?"

KOSSYPHIDIOS: "The expression 'the god' at the end of the *Crito* is indeterminate. 'The god,' in the words Plato has Socrates speak, is frequently the equivalent of 'the divine,' 'the divinity,' 'divine nature.'"

GEPHYRIOS: "However, 'the god' of the conclusion, the one Socrates acknowledges as the 'guide' for him and Crito, must be the same as the one who has, in fact, already guided him by means of the dream."

KOSSYPHIDIOS: "I'm not putting words into your mouth. But, although dreams can, in fact, be sent by more than one god, of all of these there is one particularly for whom the dream is the principal, if not the sole, means of action: Asclepius. At the beginning of our talk I innocently recalled him, but now this takes on its full meaning: on all Greek soil—Athens as well as anywhere else—a person wanting to know the cure for his disease would go to sleep in the sanctuary dedicated to Asclepius and await the dream that would dictate the appropriate behavior and cure. Socrates, a prisoner in chains, obviously was unable to go to the Asclepian cave and dream there. Asclepius, therefore, had to come to him, precisely at the moment at which Socrates would have to face his friend's final 'attack of false good sense,' and at the same time would have to cure him."

GEPHYRIOS: "Doesn't it seem curious that the master of dreams thought it a good idea to go through Socrates to tell Crito—who, although he is the only one who is sick, did not consult him—the cure for a disease that the sick man did not know he had?"

KOSSYPHIDIOS: "No doubt that is a specific quality of such friendships as this, friendships in which one of the friends is Socrates, and that even the gods themselves respect for their interdependence and unity: whatever one of them does deeply involves the other. And then Socrates himself, Socrates the just and steady, as the syllogism from our childhood reminds us, is only a mortal. Crito, as the spokesman for his devoted friends, has visited him constantly in prison, and these persistent visits are for Socrates simultaneously a repeated test and temptation (and even now, once again, ἔτι καὶ νῦν, 'let yourself be persuaded by me and secure your safety,' says the visitor). The expected assault will be the hardest of all. No matter how convinced he is, there is something within him, within this body, that the soul never completely masters, that can be seduced. Nerves and hearts have powers of their own. Even in the *Phaedo*, does he not thank his friends for the lengthy diversion with which, thanks to them, his mind was occupied during these most difficult hours?

"Although it is not contagious, Crito's 'disease,' with its repeated symptoms—the approaches, and the plan that it has inspired in him, which involves Socrates in advance—cannot help disturbing the serenity of the one who is not merely his interlocutor but who is at stake and is the substance of his unconsciously perverse conduct. Crito, as the marquise would say, hurts in his Socrates, and Socrates, doubly linked to Crito by friendship and by this sort of imperious symbiosis, cannot help feeling uncomfortable. When it comes right down to it, is he completely sure of himself? Throughout the entire visit he will have to cure his friend, but at the same time, deciding his own fate, he will have to justify his decision in his own sight one last time. For he is free in his prison, free to live or die. 'The god' and even the dream are no substitute for his will. And his refutation of Crito's arguments is only a meditation aloud, one that he could do just as easily, that he must have done more than once, alone. This is so to such an extent that, for this refutation, he imagines a second dialogue, one in which Crito has no part and in which he himself plays the role of Crito confronted by surprising interlocutors, the laws, in the role that he, Socrates, plays when faced with his friend.

"SOCRATES: 'Suppose that just as we were leaving or escaping this place, whatever you want to call it, the laws and the whole city came to confront us and said: 'Tell us, Socrates, what are you going to do? Can an action such as the one you are attempting have any intention other than to destroy us?'

"The vivid way in which he imagines himself giving in to temptation, fleeing Athens with Crito, is sufficient evidence that there is a risk of temptation. In short, 'poor judgment,' this disease of the mind, is something they both have; it is highly virulent in Crito and his friends and present as a germ in Socrates—as it is in any mortal. Asclepius answered the question—the one that it was physically impossible to ask him—by the book, because Socrates, who is the only one conscious of the disease, cannot leave prison: the prescription for a cure is to wait and accept the death set for the third day."

GEPHYRIOS: "That, in fact, explains why Socrates acknowledges himself, along with Crito and his friends, as owing the cock. But it is also conceivable that he personally never experienced any risk of contamination by Crito and that, as he often does, he is merely pretending out of courtesy and affection—or rather out of 'friendly condescension,' as our fine teacher Léon Robin called it in explaining one of the dialogues, I don't remember which—that he did run such a risk, ran it and escaped from it at the same time as he did, thus contracting the same debt as Crito's toward the god."

KOSSYPHIDIOS: "That is certainly possible. Something even more profound is also conceivable: the mix of temporal friendship and philosophical love discussed in the *Phaedrus*, one that makes the persons touched by it inseparable. We said just now that Crito hurt in his Socrates; Socrates too hurts in his Crito. Whatever the case may be, whether subtly or not, we have accounted for the confusion of numbers and persons in the eleven Greek words that are the last words of Socrates. Here is what they say: 'Crito, the other morning, we—you and I and through you all of our friends—received in my dream the advice that put an end to the disease of your minds and the intellectual and sentimental effects they had, or risked having, on mine. We consequently owe the god of healing the cock in payment for cures. Pay, do not forget!'"

GEPHYRIOS: "You have convinced me. How much better I like this message. It is so simple and so rich in the Greek, or in the Latin of Marsilio Ficino, which is no less simple: 'O Crito, Aesculapio gallum debemus, quem reddite neque neglegatis.' And I understand better the grave overtones in Crito's reply and his last question, which will remain unanswered: 'Fiet, inquit Crito, quod jubes. Sed vide num quid aliud velis?' Haec interroganti nihil ultra respondit."*

* "What you command shall be done, said Crito. But is there anything else you wish? To these questions he made no further reply." [Trans.]

KOSSYPHIDIOS: "I am not going to let you have the last word, my friend—neither you nor Crito. There remains one point worth emphasizing. Sometimes it may seem astonishing that, after having tossed around great ideas all afternoon, Socrates devotes his last wisp of breath to the words recalling this debt: could he not have mentioned it earlier? But, to the contrary: how perfectly appropriate! Lucid to the last, Socrates waited for the ultimate limit, the conclusive moment, what we used to call in the cave 'being on the point of death,' to state officially that the god had fulfilled his contract and, having not deceived him, deserved the cock: already this is the voice of the dead man registering his death—now no longer reversible by the voice of the man who is dying. He has no time to explain to Crito or his sorrowful friends; he has just enough time to bring things to a close. It is up to them to understand, to confirm how right he was: nihil ultra respondit, sed cum parvo tempore interquievit, commotus est. Et minister detexit eum atque ipse lumina fixit. Quod cum Crito cerneret, ora oculosque composuit."*

Where I am sending you this report from, my dear François, is something I do not know. From the beyond, where I have remained, perhaps? From my Vexin, where I might have returned? My interlocutors and my guide, your father, left me alone and, though I was asleep already, satisfied and replete, I fell asleep again: asleep asleep. Which waking is this? In any case, I have no doubt that this letter will reach you, either by post or by ghost.

* "He made no further reply, but after a bit of time passed, he shook. The attendant uncovered him and his eyes were fixed. Therefore Crito made the decision; he arranged his eyes and mouth." [Trans.]